99 Advanced Programming Algorithms Handbook With Python

Jamie Flux

https://www.linkedin.com/company/golden-dawn-engineering/

Collaborate with Us!

Have an innovative business idea or a project you'd like to
collaborate on?
We're always eager to explore new opportunities for growth and
partnership.
Please feel free to reach out to us at:

https://www.linkedin.com/company/golden-dawn-
engineering/

We look forward to hearing from you!

Contents

Chapter 1

Suffix Trees: Linear-Time Construction and Applications

Below is a Python code snippet that encompasses the core computational elements related to suffix trees, including construction using Ukkonen's algorithm and application for string matching.

```python
class SuffixTree:
    class Node:
        def __init__(self, start, end):
            self.start = start
            self.end = end
            self.suffix_link = None
            self.children = {}

    def __init__(self, text):
        self.text = text
        self.n = len(text)
        self.root = self.Node(-1, -1)
        self.build_suffix_tree()

    def build_suffix_tree(self):
        # Active variables to track the construction process
        active_node = self.root
        active_edge = -1
        active_length = 0
```

```python
remainder = 0
last_new_node = None

for pos in range(self.n):
    remainder += 1
    last_new_node = None

    while remainder > 0:
        if active_length == 0:  # Active length being zero
        ↪   means need to reset active_edge
            active_edge = pos

        if self.text[active_edge] not in
        ↪   active_node.children:
            active_node.children[self.text[active_edge]] =
            ↪   self.Node(pos, self.n)
            if last_new_node:
                last_new_node.suffix_link = active_node
                last_new_node = None
        else:
            next_node =
            ↪   active_node.children[self.text[active_edge]]
            edge_length = next_node.end - next_node.start

            if active_length >= edge_length:
                active_edge += edge_length
                active_length -= edge_length
                active_node = next_node
                continue

            if self.text[next_node.start + active_length] ==
            ↪   self.text[pos]:
                active_length += 1
                if last_new_node:
                    last_new_node.suffix_link = active_node
                    last_new_node = None
                break

            split_end = next_node.start + active_length
            split_node = self.Node(next_node.start,
            ↪   split_end)
            active_node.children[self.text[active_edge]] =
            ↪   split_node
            split_node.children[self.text[pos]] =
            ↪   self.Node(pos, self.n)

            next_node.start = split_end
            split_node.children[self.text[split_end]] =
            ↪   next_node

            if last_new_node:
                last_new_node.suffix_link = split_node
```

```
                    last_new_node = split_node

                remainder -= 1

                if active_node == self.root and active_length > 0:
                    active_length -= 1
                    active_edge = pos - remainder + 1
                elif active_node != self.root:
                    active_node = active_node.suffix_link if
                    ↪ active_node.suffix_link else self.root

    def search(self, pattern):
        current_node = self.root
        match_length = 0
        for char in pattern:
            if match_length == 0:
                if char in current_node.children:
                    match_node = current_node.children[char]
                    match_length = match_node.end - match_node.start
                else:
                    return False
            if self.text[match_node.start + match_length -
            ↪ (match_node.end - match_node.start)] == char:
                match_length -= 1
                if match_length == 0:
                    current_node = match_node
            else:
                return False
        return True

# Example Usage
st = SuffixTree("banana")
assert st.search("ana") is True
assert st.search("nana") is True
assert st.search("bana") is False
```

This code defines several key functions and classes necessary for the construction and utilization of a suffix tree:

- The `SuffixTree` class initializes with a string and constructs the suffix tree using Ukkonen's algorithm.

- The node class `Node` stores information about the start and end indices of the substring and children nodes.

- `build_suffix_tree` constructs the suffix tree in linear time by maintaining active variables and handling suffix links.

- `search` function checks if a given pattern exists in the tree, verifying efficient substring matching.

The final block provides examples of constructing a suffix tree for the string "banana" and performing search operations.

Chapter 2

Suffix Arrays and Enhanced Suffix Arrays

Below is a Python code snippet that illustrates the construction of a suffix array using the efficient DC3 (Difference Cover) or Skew algorithm and enhances it for full-text indexing applications by implementing a simple form of longest common prefix (LCP) array construction.

```python
def sort_cyclic_shifts(s):
    n = len(s)
    alphabet = sorted(set(s))
    p = [0] * n
    c = [0] * n
    count = {char: 0 for char in alphabet}

    for char in s:
        count[char] += 1
    char_idx = {char: idx for idx, char in enumerate(alphabet)}

    for i in range(1, len(alphabet)):
        count[alphabet[i]] += count[alphabet[i - 1]]
    for i in range(n):
        count[s[i]] -= 1
        p[count[s[i]]] = i
    classes = 1
    c[p[0]] = 0

    for i in range(1, n):
        if s[p[i]] != s[p[i - 1]]:
            classes += 1
        c[p[i]] = classes - 1
```

```python
    pn = [0] * n
    cn = [0] * n
    h = 0
    while (1 << h) < n:
        for i in range(n):
            pn[i] = p[i] - (1 << h)
            if pn[i] < 0:
                pn[i] += n
        count = [0] * classes
        for i in range(n):
            count[c[pn[i]]] += 1
        for i in range(1, classes):
            count[i] += count[i - 1]
        for i in range(n-1, -1, -1):
            count[c[pn[i]]] -= 1
            p[count[c[pn[i]]]] = pn[i]

        cn[p[0]] = 0
        classes = 1
        for i in range(1, n):
            curr = (c[p[i]], c[(p[i] + (1 << h)) % n])
            prev = (c[p[i - 1]], c[(p[i - 1] + (1 << h)) % n])
            if curr != prev:
                classes += 1
            cn[p[i]] = classes - 1
        c, cn = cn, c
        h += 1
    return p


def suffix_array_construction(s):
    s += '$'
    return sort_cyclic_shifts(s)


def lcp_array_construction(s, p):
    n = len(s)
    rank = [0] * n
    lcp = [0] * (n - 1)

    for i, suffix_index in enumerate(p):
        rank[suffix_index] = i

    h = 0
    for i in range(n):
        if rank[i] > 0:
            j = p[rank[i] - 1]
            while i + h < n and j + h < n and s[i + h] == s[j + h]:
                h += 1
            lcp[rank[i] - 1] = h
            if h > 0:
                h -= 1
    return lcp
```

```
# Example usage:
text = "banana"
suffix_array = suffix_array_construction(text)
lcp_array = lcp_array_construction(text + '$', suffix_array)

# Outputs for demonstration
print("Suffix Array:", suffix_array)
print("LCP Array:", lcp_array)
```

This code provides an efficient method to construct the suffix array and LCP array for a given text:

- `sort_cyclic_shifts` function uses the DC3 or Skew algorithm to sort cyclic shifts of a string, resulting in a suffix array.

- `suffix_array_construction` builds the suffix array by appending a sentinel character to the input string.

- `lcp_array_construction` calculates the Longest Common Prefix (LCP) array using the constructed suffix array and string ranks.

These data structures are instrumental for full-text indexing and solving string-related computational problems efficiently.

Chapter 3

Knuth-Morris-Pratt (KMP) Pattern Matching Algorithm

Below is a Python code snippet that encompasses the core computational elements of the Knuth-Morris-Pratt (KMP) pattern matching algorithm, including the preprocessing of the pattern to build the failure function and the pattern searching procedure in the text.

```python
def compute_failure_function(pattern):
    """
    Compute the failure function for the KMP algorithm.

    :param pattern: The pattern string to preprocess.
    :return: The list representing the failure function.
    """
    m = len(pattern)
    failure = [0] * m  # Initialize the failure function array
    j = 0  # Length of the previous longest prefix suffix

    # Start from the second character in the pattern
    for i in range(1, m):
        while j > 0 and pattern[i] != pattern[j]:
            j = failure[j - 1]  # Get the previous position from
            ↪    failure function

        if pattern[i] == pattern[j]:
            j += 1

        failure[i] = j
```

```
        return failure

def kmp_search(text, pattern):
    """
    Perform KMP pattern matching to find occurrences of a pattern in
    ↪   a text.

    :param text: The text string to search within.
    :param pattern: The pattern string to search for.
    :return: A list of starting indices where the pattern is found
    ↪   in the text.
    """
    n = len(text)
    m = len(pattern)
    failure = compute_failure_function(pattern)
    result = []

    j = 0  # Index for pattern[] (also used for text)

    # Traverse the text
    for i in range(n):
        while j > 0 and text[i] != pattern[j]:
            j = failure[j - 1]  # Use failure function to shift the
            ↪   pattern

        if text[i] == pattern[j]:
            j += 1

        if j == m:
            result.append(i - m + 1)  # Found a match, record the
            ↪   start index
            j = failure[j - 1]  # Prepare for the next potential
            ↪   match

    return result

# Example usage
text = "ababcabcabababd"
pattern = "ababd"
matches = kmp_search(text, pattern)

print("Pattern found at indices:", matches)
```

This code defines key functions necessary for implementing the
KMP algorithm for efficient pattern searching in strings:

- `compute_failure_function` preprocesses the pattern to construct the failure function, which is used to skip unnecessary
  comparisons during the search.

- `kmp_search` performs the actual search in the given text using the precomputed failure function to efficiently locate all

16

occurrences of the pattern.

The final block provides an example of how the implemented KMP algorithm can be used to find a pattern within a text string, demonstrating its effectiveness and efficiency.

Chapter 4

Boyer-Moore String Search Algorithm

Below is a Python code snippet that provides a comprehensive implementation of the Boyer-Moore string search algorithm, including the construction of the bad character rule and good suffix rule tables for efficient pattern matching in text.

```python
def boyer_moore_search(text, pattern):
    """
    Perform Boyer-Moore pattern matching algorithm on the given text
    ↪    and pattern.
    :param text: The text in which to search.
    :param pattern: The pattern to search for.
    :return: A list of starting indices where pattern is found in
    ↪    text.
    """
    def bad_character_table(pattern):
        """
        Create the bad character shift table.
        :param pattern: The pattern for which to create the table.
        :return: A dictionary with the last occurrence of each
        ↪    character in the pattern.
        """
        bad_char_table = {}
        pattern_length = len(pattern)
        for index, char in enumerate(pattern):
            bad_char_table[char] = pattern_length - index - 1
        return bad_char_table

    def good_suffix_table(pattern):
        """
        Create the good suffix shift table.
```

```python
    :param pattern: The pattern for which to create the table.
    :return: A list of shifts corresponding to suffixes of the
    ↪   pattern.
    """
    pattern_length = len(pattern)
    good_suffix_shift = [0] * (pattern_length + 1)
    border_pos = pattern_length
    bpos = [0] * (pattern_length + 1)
    bpos[border_pos] = border_pos + 1
    shift = [0] * (pattern_length + 1)

    for i in range(pattern_length - 1, -1, -1):
        while (border_pos < pattern_length and pattern[i] !=
        ↪   pattern[border_pos]):
            if (shift[border_pos] == 0):
                shift[border_pos] = border_pos - i
            border_pos = bpos[border_pos]
        border_pos -= 1
        bpos[i] = border_pos

    border_pos = bpos[0]
    for i in range(pattern_length):
        if (shift[i] == 0):
            shift[i] = border_pos
        if (i == border_pos):
            border_pos = bpos[border_pos]

    for i in range(pattern_length + 1):
        good_suffix_shift[i] = shift[i]

    return good_suffix_shift

def preprocess_tables(pattern):
    """
    Preprocess the bad character and good suffix tables.
    :param pattern: The pattern for which to preprocess the
    ↪   tables.
    :return: The bad character and good suffix tables.
    """
    bad_char_table = bad_character_table(pattern)
    good_suffix_table_values = good_suffix_table(pattern)
    return bad_char_table, good_suffix_table_values

bad_char_table, good_suffix_table_values =
↪   preprocess_tables(pattern)
text_length = len(text)
pattern_length = len(pattern)
indices = []
offset = 0

while offset <= text_length - pattern_length:
    scan_index = pattern_length - 1
```

19

```
    while scan_index >= 0 and pattern[scan_index] == text[offset
↪    + scan_index]:
        scan_index -= 1

    if scan_index < 0:
        indices.append(offset)
        offset += good_suffix_table_values[0]
    else:
        bad_char_shift = bad_char_table.get(text[offset +
↪    scan_index], pattern_length)
        good_suffix_shift = good_suffix_table_values[scan_index
↪    + 1]
        offset += max(bad_char_shift, good_suffix_shift)

return indices

# Example usage
text = "here is a simple example"
pattern = "example"
matches = boyer_moore_search(text, pattern)
print("Pattern found at indices:", matches)
```

This code implements the Boyer-Moore algorithm for pattern matching as follows:

- `boyer_moore_search` function orchestrates the Boyer-Moore search process on the given text and pattern.

- `bad_character_table` constructs the bad character table to facilitate quick character mismatch handling.

- `good_suffix_table` generates shifts for pattern substrings aligned with suffixes in pattern.

- `preprocess_tables` preprocesses both bad character and good suffix tables for the search algorithm.

- The example usage demonstrates how to utilize the `boyer_moore_search` function to locate a pattern in a given text.

Chapter 5

Rabin-Karp Algorithm for Multiple Pattern Search

Below is a Python code snippet implementing the Rabin-Karp algorithm for multi-pattern string searching. It utilizes rolling hash functions and handles collision resolution.

```python
def rabin_karp_multi_pattern_search(text, patterns):
    '''
    Implements the Rabin-Karp algorithm for searching multiple
    ↪   patterns in a text.
    :param text: The text to search within.
    :param patterns: A list of patterns to search for.
    :return: A dictionary with patterns as keys and lists of start
    ↪   indices as values.
    '''
    def rolling_hash(old_hash, old_char, new_char, base, modulus):
        '''
        Updates hash by removing the old_char, adding new_char using
        ↪   the base and modulus.
        '''
        return (old_hash * base - ord(old_char) * high_order +
        ↪   ord(new_char)) % modulus

    def initial_hash(s, length, base, modulus):
        '''
        Computes the initial hash for a substring of given length.
        '''
        return sum(ord(s[i]) * (base ** (length - i - 1)) for i in
        ↪   range(length)) % modulus
```

```python
# Define base and modulus for hashing
base, modulus = 256, 1000000007

# Precompute the high order digit value
high_order = base ** (max(len(pattern) for pattern in patterns)
↪   - 1) % modulus

results = {pattern: [] for pattern in patterns}

for pattern in patterns:
    m = len(pattern)
    pattern_hash = initial_hash(pattern, m, base, modulus)
    current_hash = initial_hash(text, m, base, modulus)

    for i in range(len(text) - m + 1):
        if current_hash == pattern_hash:
            # Potential match found, perform a direct check
            if text[i:i+m] == pattern:
                results[pattern].append(i)

        if i < len(text) - m:
            # Roll the hash over to the next substring
            current_hash = rolling_hash(current_hash, text[i],
↪   text[i+m], base, modulus)
            if current_hash < 0:
                current_hash += modulus

    return results

# Example Usage
text = "abracadabra"
patterns = ["abra", "cad"]
found_positions = rabin_karp_multi_pattern_search(text, patterns)

print("Pattern occurrences:", found_positions)
```

The provided Python code implements several key features of
the Rabin-Karp algorithm for multi-pattern search:

- `rabin_karp_multi_pattern_search` function conducts the
  search for multiple patterns within a given text.

- `rolling_hash` updates the hash value by sliding the window
  across the text efficiently.

- `initial_hash` calculates the hash for the initial window of
  text.

- The function returns a dictionary where each pattern maps
  to a list of starting indices where it is found in the text.

This implementation efficiently handles hashing of patterns using a base and modulus, addresses potential hash collisions, and iterates over the text to find occurrences of each pattern.

Chapter 6

Aho-Corasick Algorithm for Pattern Matching

Below is a Python code snippet that implements the Aho-Corasick algorithm for searching multiple patterns in a text. It includes functionalities such as trie construction, failure links, and output functions for efficient matching.

```python
class AhoCorasick:
    def __init__(self):
        self.num_states = 1
        self.trie = [{'next': {}, 'fail': 0, 'output': []}]  #
        ↪    Initialize the trie

    def add_word(self, word, index):
        current_state = 0
        for char in word:
            if char not in self.trie[current_state]['next']:
                self.trie[current_state]['next'][char] =
                ↪    self.num_states
                self.trie.append({'next': {}, 'fail': 0, 'output':
                ↪    []})
                self.num_states += 1
            current_state = self.trie[current_state]['next'][char]
        self.trie[current_state]['output'].append(index)

    def build_failure_links(self):
        from collections import deque
        queue = deque()
```

```
        # BFS for constructing fail links
        for char, nxt_state in self.trie[0]['next'].items():
            queue.append(nxt_state)
            self.trie[nxt_state]['fail'] = 0

        while queue:
            state = queue.popleft()
            for char, next_state in
            ↪   self.trie[state]['next'].items():
                queue.append(next_state)
                fail_state = self.trie[state]['fail']
                while char not in self.trie[fail_state]['next'] and
                ↪   fail_state != 0:
                    fail_state = self.trie[fail_state]['fail']
                self.trie[next_state]['fail'] =
                ↪   self.trie[fail_state]['next'].get(char, 0)
                self.trie[next_state]['output'] +=
                ↪   self.trie[self.trie[next_state]['fail']]['output']

    def search(self, text):
        current_state = 0
        results = []
        for i, char in enumerate(text):
            while char not in self.trie[current_state]['next'] and
            ↪   current_state != 0:
                current_state = self.trie[current_state]['fail']
            current_state =
            ↪   self.trie[current_state]['next'].get(char, 0)
            for pattern_id in self.trie[current_state]['output']:
                results.append((i, pattern_id))
        return results

# Example usage
patterns = ["he", "she", "his", "hers"]
ac = AhoCorasick()
for index, pattern in enumerate(patterns):
    ac.add_word(pattern, index)
ac.build_failure_links()
text = "ushers"
matches = ac.search(text)

print("Matches found:", matches)
```

This code defines several key components necessary for the Aho-Corasick algorithm:

- The `AhoCorasick` class is the core structure that holds the algorithm's state.

- `add_word` method adds words to the trie and associates them with pattern indices for easy identification.

- **build_failure_links** method constructs the failure links using breadth-first search to ensure efficient backtracking.

- **search** method runs the text through the constructed automaton, offering a list of matches with their positions.

The final block of code provides an example of how to utilize the Aho-Corasick algorithm to find occurrences of multiple patterns in a given text.

Chapter 7

Z-Algorithm for Pattern Searching

Below is a Python code snippet that implements the Z-algorithm which is used for pattern matching and string preprocessing by computing the Z-array to identify pattern occurrences.

```python
def calculate_z_array(s):
    '''
    Calculate the Z-array for a given string.
    :param s: Input string.
    :return: Z-array where each element represents the length of the
    ↪ longest substring
            starting from that position which is also a prefix of
            ↪ s.
    '''
    Z = [0] * len(s)
    L, R, K = 0, 0, 0
    for i in range(1, len(s)):
        if i > R:
            L, R = i, i
            while R < len(s) and s[R] == s[R - L]:
                R += 1
            Z[i] = R - L
            R -= 1
        else:
            K = i - L
            if Z[K] < R - i + 1:
                Z[i] = Z[K]
            else:
                L = i
                while R < len(s) and s[R] == s[R - L]:
                    R += 1
```

```
                Z[i] = R - L
                R -= 1
        return Z

def z_algorithm(pattern, text):
    '''
    Finds occurrences of a pattern in a text using the Z-algorithm.
    :param pattern: The pattern to search for.
    :param text: The text to search within.
    :return: Positions where the pattern occurs in the text.
    '''
    concatenated = pattern + "$" + text
    Z = calculate_z_array(concatenated)
    occurrences = []
    pattern_length = len(pattern)

    for i in range(len(Z)):
        if Z[i] == pattern_length:
            occurrences.append(i - pattern_length - 1)

    return occurrences

# Example usage
pattern = "abc"
text = "abcpqrabcxyz"
print("Pattern found at indices:", z_algorithm(pattern, text))
```

This code defines essential components of the Z-algorithm:

- `calculate_z_array` function computes the Z-array where each element $Z[i]$ stores the length of the longest substring starting from the ith position that is also a prefix of the input string.

- `z_algorithm` leverages the Z-array to find all positions where the input pattern occurs in the text. It concatenates the pattern and the text with a unique delimiter to prevent overlap issues.

The final block demonstrates the code's execution, showing how the Z-algorithm can be used to detect pattern occurrences within a given text.

Chapter 8

Manacher's Algorithm for Longest Palindromic Substring

Below is a Python code snippet that implements Manacher's algorithm for finding the longest palindromic substring in linear time. This implementation includes string transformation and calculation of palindrome radii.

```python
def preprocess_string(s):
    """
    Preprocess the original string by inserting '#' between each
    ↪    character
    and adding sentinel characters '^' at the start and '$' at the
    ↪    end.
    :param s: Original string.
    :return: Transformed string with added special characters.
    """
    return '^#' + '#'.join(s) + '#$'

def manachers_algorithm(s):
    """
    Manacher's Algorithm to find the longest palindromic substring.
    :param s: Original input string.
    :return: The longest palindromic substring.
    """
    T = preprocess_string(s)
    n = len(T)
    P = [0] * n   # Palindrome radius array
    C = 0   # Center of the current right-most palindrome
    R = 0   # Right edge of the current right-most palindrome
```

```
for i in range(1, n - 1):
    mirr = 2 * C - i  # Mirror of the current position i

    if i < R:
        P[i] = min(R - i, P[mirr])  # Use previously computed
        ↪  values

    # Attempt to expand the palindrome centered at i
    while T[i + P[i] + 1] == T[i - P[i] - 1]:
        P[i] += 1

    # Adjust the center and right edge if expanded beyond R
    if i + P[i] > R:
        C, R = i, i + P[i]

# Find the maximum palindrome length and its center
max_len, center_index = max((n, i) for i, n in enumerate(P))
start = (center_index - max_len) // 2  # Start index in the
↪  original string

return s[start:start + max_len]
```

```
# Example usage
original_string = "forgeeksskeegfor"
longest_palindrome = manachers_algorithm(original_string)
print("Longest Palindrome Substring:", longest_palindrome)
```

This code defines functions necessary for efficiently finding the longest palindromic substring in a given string:

- **preprocess_string** function transforms the input string by adding delimiters to handle even-length palindromes uniformly, preventing index overflow during palindrome expansion.

- **manachers_algorithm** implements the core logic of Manacher's algorithm, maintaining a record of palindrome radii, dynamically adjusting the center as the palindrome expands past its known boundary.

- The calculation of the actual longest palindromic substring uses the precomputed palindrome radii to extract and reconstruct the result from the original input.

The final section provides an example of how the algorithm would locate and return the longest palindromic substring within a sample string.

Chapter 9

Suffix Automata: Construction and Applications

Below is a Python code snippet that encompasses the core operations for constructing and utilizing a suffix automaton. This structure is used for efficient representation and querying of substrings.

```python
class SuffixAutomaton:
    def __init__(self, s):
        '''
        Initialize the suffix automaton for the given string.
        :param s: Input string for the automaton.
        '''
        self.size = 1
        self.last = 0
        self.max_len = [0] * (2 * len(s))
        self.link = [-1] * (2 * len(s))
        self.next = [{} for _ in range(2 * len(s))]
        self.build(s)

    def build(self, s):
        '''
        Construct the suffix automaton using the input string.
        :param s: Input string for the automaton.
        '''
        for character in s:
            self.add_char(character)

    def add_char(self, c):
```

```
    '''
    Add a character to the suffix automaton.
    :param c: The character to add.
    '''
    current = self.size
    self.size += 1
    self.max_len[current] = self.max_len[self.last] + 1
    p = self.last
    while p != -1 and c not in self.next[p]:
        self.next[p][c] = current
        p = self.link[p]
    if p == -1:
        self.link[current] = 0
    else:
        q = self.next[p][c]
        if self.max_len[p] + 1 == self.max_len[q]:
            self.link[current] = q
        else:
            clone = self.size
            self.size += 1
            self.max_len[clone] = self.max_len[p] + 1
            self.next[clone] = self.next[q].copy()
            self.link[clone] = self.link[q]
            while p != -1 and self.next[p].get(c) == q:
                self.next[p][c] = clone
                p = self.link[p]
            self.link[q] = self.link[current] = clone
    self.last = current

def longest_common_substring(self, other):
    '''
    Find the longest common substring between the automaton's
    ↪  string and another string.
    :param other: Another string for comparison.
    :return: Length and ending index of the longest common
    ↪  substring.
    '''
    current = length = best = 0
    best_pos = 0
    for i, c in enumerate(other):
        while current != -1 and c not in self.next[current]:
            current = self.link[current]
            length = self.max_len[current] if current != -1 else
            ↪  0
        if current == -1:
            current = length = 0
            continue
        current = self.next[current][c]
        length += 1
        if length > best:
            best = length
            best_pos = i
    return best, best_pos - best + 1
```

```
# Example usage:
s1 = "abacabadabacaba"
s2 = "dabac"
sa = SuffixAutomaton(s1)
length, position = sa.longest_common_substring(s2)
print(f"Longest common substring length: {length}, position in
↪    second string: {position}")
```

This code defines several key components necessary for creating
and utilizing a suffix automaton efficiently:

- `SuffixAutomaton` class initialization constructs the data structure's basics based on the input string.

- `build` and `add_char` methods are used iteratively to construct the automaton by adding each character of the string.

- `longest_common_substring` function identifies and returns the longest common substring between the input string and another string using the automaton.

The final block of code gives an example of constructing a suffix automaton for a string and finding the longest common substring with a second string.

Chapter 10

Viterbi Algorithm for Hidden Markov Models

Below is a Python code snippet that implements the Viterbi algorithm for decoding the most probable sequence of hidden states in Hidden Markov Models (HMM), with applications in fields like speech recognition and bioinformatics.

```python
import numpy as np

def viterbi_algorithm(observations, states, start_prob, trans_prob,
↪    emit_prob):
    """
    Implementation of the Viterbi algorithm for decoding the most
    ↪    probable sequence of states.

    :param observations: List of observations (e.g., in speech
    ↪    recognition, these might be acoustic signals).
    :param states: List of possible states in the HMM.
    :param start_prob: A dictionary with starting probabilities of
    ↪    each state.
    :param trans_prob: A dictionary with transition probabilities
    ↪    between states.
    :param emit_prob: A dictionary with emission probabilities of
    ↪    observations from states.
    :return: A tuple containing the most probable state sequence and
    ↪    the probability of that sequence.
    """
    # Initialization
    n_obs = len(observations)
    n_states = len(states)
    V = np.zeros((n_states, n_obs))
    path = np.zeros((n_states, n_obs), dtype=int)
```

```python
    # Initialize base cases (t == 0)
    for i in range(n_states):
        V[i, 0] = start_prob[states[i]] *
        ↪    emit_prob[states[i]].get(observations[0], 0)
        path[i, 0] = i

    # Run Viterbi algorithm for t > 0
    for t in range(1, n_obs):
        new_path = np.zeros((n_states, n_obs), dtype=int)
        for y in range(n_states):
            (prob, state) = max(
                (V[y0, t - 1] *
                ↪    trans_prob[states[y0]].get(states[y], 0) *
                ↪    emit_prob[states[y]].get(observations[t], 0),
                ↪    y0)
                for y0 in range(n_states))
            V[y, t] = prob
            new_path[y, :t] = path[state, :t]
            new_path[y, t] = y

        # Update the path
        path = new_path

    # Find the most probable last state
    (prob, state) = max((V[y, n_obs - 1], y) for y in
    ↪    range(n_states))

    # Return the most probable path and its probability
    return (path[state], prob)

# Define states and possible observations
states = ('Healthy', 'Fever')
observations = ('normal', 'cold', 'dizzy')
start_probability = {'Healthy': 0.6, 'Fever': 0.4}
transition_probability = {
    'Healthy' : {'Healthy': 0.7, 'Fever': 0.3},
    'Fever' : {'Healthy': 0.4, 'Fever': 0.6}
}
emission_probability = {
    'Healthy' : {'normal': 0.5, 'cold': 0.4, 'dizzy': 0.1},
    'Fever' : {'normal': 0.1, 'cold': 0.3, 'dizzy': 0.6}
}

# Execute Viterbi algorithm
optimal_path, path_prob = viterbi_algorithm(observations, states,
↪    start_probability, transition_probability, emission_probability)

# Map state indices to state names
optimal_state_sequence = [states[state] for state in optimal_path]

print("Most probable state sequence:", optimal_state_sequence)
```

```
print("Probability of this sequence:", path_prob)
```

This code defines the implementation of the Viterbi algorithm for determining the most probable sequence of hidden states given a sequence of observations and a Hidden Markov Model:

- `viterbi_algorithm` function computes the most probable sequence of states ("Healthy," "Fever") given a set of observations ("normal," "cold," "dizzy").

- It initializes the Viterbi likelihood table and recursively updates it based on transition and emission probabilities.

- The final step extracts the optimal state sequence and its associated probability.

The code demonstrates an application where the hidden states represent health conditions and observations relate to symptoms, showcasing the power of HMM in decoding sequence data.

Chapter 11

Needleman-Wunsch Algorithm for Global Sequence Alignment

Below is a Python code snippet that implements the Needleman-Wunsch algorithm for optimal global alignment of sequences using dynamic programming matrices and scoring schemes.

```python
def needleman_wunsch(seq1, seq2, match_score=1, gap_cost=1):
    """
    Perform global alignment using the Needleman-Wunsch algorithm.
    :param seq1: First sequence.
    :param seq2: Second sequence.
    :param match_score: Score for character match.
    :param gap_cost: Cost for gaps.
    :return: Tuple of aligned sequences and alignment score.
    """
    n = len(seq1)
    m = len(seq2)

    # Initialize scoring matrix
    score_matrix = [[0] * (m + 1) for _ in range(n + 1)]

    # Fill scoring matrix
    for i in range(1, n + 1):
        score_matrix[i][0] = i * -gap_cost
    for j in range(1, m + 1):
        score_matrix[0][j] = j * -gap_cost

    # Populate rest of the matrix
    for i in range(1, n + 1):
```

```python
    for j in range(1, m + 1):
        match = score_matrix[i-1][j-1] + (match_score if
        ↪  seq1[i-1] == seq2[j-1] else -match_score)
        delete = score_matrix[i-1][j] - gap_cost
        insert = score_matrix[i][j-1] - gap_cost
        score_matrix[i][j] = max(match, delete, insert)

# Traceback to get alignments
align1, align2 = "", ""
i, j = n, m
while i > 0 and j > 0:
    current_score = score_matrix[i][j]
    if current_score == score_matrix[i-1][j-1] + (match_score if
    ↪  seq1[i-1] == seq2[j-1] else -match_score):
        align1 = seq1[i-1] + align1
        align2 = seq2[j-1] + align2
        i -= 1
        j -= 1
    elif current_score == score_matrix[i-1][j] - gap_cost:
        align1 = seq1[i-1] + align1
        align2 = '-' + align2
        i -= 1
    else:
        align1 = '-' + align1
        align2 = seq2[j-1] + align2
        j -= 1

# Add remaining gaps for remaining characters
while i > 0:
    align1 = seq1[i-1] + align1
    align2 = '-' + align2
    i -= 1

while j > 0:
    align1 = '-' + align1
    align2 = seq2[j-1] + align2
    j -= 1

score = score_matrix[n][m]
return align1, align2, score

# Example usage
seq1 = "GATTACA"
seq2 = "GCATGCU"
alignment = needleman_wunsch(seq1, seq2)
print(f"Alignment 1: {alignment[0]}")
print(f"Alignment 2: {alignment[1]}")
print(f"Alignment Score: {alignment[2]}")
```

This Python code describes the implementation of the global alignment algorithm using a dynamic programming approach:

- The `needleman_wunsch` function sets up a scoring matrix to evaluate the best alignment.

- Score calculations consider matches, deletions, and insertions, accounting for specified match and gap costs.

- The traceback step reconstructs the optimal alignment based on the highest accumulated scores.

- `seq1` and `seq2` are example input sequences used to demonstrate the algorithm's capability to deduce an optimal alignment and score.

Chapter 12

Smith-Waterman Algorithm for Local Sequence Alignment

Below is a Python code snippet that implements the Smith-Waterman algorithm for local sequence alignment. The code initializes a scoring matrix, performs dynamic programming to compute scores, and traces back the optimal local alignment.

```python
def smith_waterman(seq1, seq2, match_score=2, gap_cost=1,
↪   mismatch_cost=1):
    """
    Compute the Smith-Waterman alignment between two sequences.
    :param seq1: First sequence.
    :param seq2: Second sequence.
    :param match_score: Score for matches.
    :param gap_cost: Cost for gaps.
    :param mismatch_cost: Cost for mismatches.
    :return: Best alignment score and the aligned sequences.
    """
    m, n = len(seq1), len(seq2)

    # Initialize scoring matrix
    score_matrix = [[0] * (n + 1) for _ in range(m + 1)]
    max_score = 0
    max_pos = (0, 0)

    # Fill scoring matrix
    for i in range(1, m + 1):
        for j in range(1, n + 1):
```

```
                    match = score_matrix[i - 1][j - 1] + (match_score if
                    ↪  seq1[i - 1] == seq2[j - 1] else -mismatch_cost)
                    delete = score_matrix[i - 1][j] - gap_cost
                    insert = score_matrix[i][j - 1] - gap_cost
                    score = max(0, match, delete, insert)  # Only keep
                    ↪  positive scores
                    score_matrix[i][j] = score
                    if score > max_score:
                        max_score = score
                        max_pos = (i, j)

        # Traceback to get the best local alignment
        aligned_1, aligned_2 = [], []
        i, j = max_pos

        while score_matrix[i][j] != 0:
            current_score = score_matrix[i][j]
            diagonal_score = score_matrix[i - 1][j - 1]
            up_score = score_matrix[i][j - 1]
            left_score = score_matrix[i - 1][j]

            if current_score == diagonal_score + (match_score if seq1[i
            ↪  - 1] == seq2[j - 1] else -mismatch_cost):
                aligned_1.append(seq1[i - 1])
                aligned_2.append(seq2[j - 1])
                i -= 1
                j -= 1
            elif current_score == left_score - gap_cost:
                aligned_1.append(seq1[i - 1])
                aligned_2.append('-')
                i -= 1
            elif current_score == up_score - gap_cost:
                aligned_1.append('-')
                aligned_2.append(seq2[j - 1])
                j -= 1

        aligned_1 = ''.join(reversed(aligned_1))
        aligned_2 = ''.join(reversed(aligned_2))

        return max_score, aligned_1, aligned_2

# Example usage
seq1 = "ACACACTA"
seq2 = "AGCACACA"
score, alignment_1, alignment_2 = smith_waterman(seq1, seq2)

print("Best Score:", score)
print("Alignment 1:", alignment_1)
print("Alignment 2:", alignment_2)
```

This code defines several key functions necessary for implementing the Smith-Waterman algorithm:

- The function `smith_waterman` computes the alignment of two sequences using scoring based on matches, mismatches, and gap penalties.

- It constructs a scoring matrix where each cell contains the maximum score possible at that position, considering matches and gaps.

- The traceback process identifies the optimal local alignment by following the path of scores back to their source, starting from the cell with the highest score.

- The aligned sequences are returned after the trace, showing the optimal local alignment with possible gaps.

Chapter 13

CYK Algorithm for Parsing Context-Free Grammars

Below is a Python code snippet that demonstrates the implementation of the CYK algorithm for parsing strings within context-free grammars, a fundamental concept in syntax analysis and computational linguistics.

```python
import numpy as np

def cyk_algorithm(grammar, string):
    """
    Implements the CYK algorithm to determine if a given string can
    ↪ be generated by a context-free grammar.

    :param grammar: A context-free grammar in Chomsky Normal Form
    ↪ (CNF).
                    Example format: {'A': [('B', 'C'), ('a',)]}
    :param string: The input string to parse.
    :return:       Boolean value indicating if the string can be
    ↪ generated by the grammar.
    """

    # Length of the input string
    n = len(string)

    # Variables used in the grammar
    variables = list(grammar.keys())

    # Initialize the parse table
```

```python
    parse_table = np.full((n, n, len(variables)), False, dtype=bool)

    # Fill the diagonal of the parse table with terminal rules
    for i in range(n):
        for var, productions in grammar.items():
            for production in productions:
                if len(production) == 1 and production[0] ==
                ↪   string[i]:
                    parse_table[i, i, variables.index(var)] = True

    # Fill the rest of the parse table
    for length in range(2, n + 1):  # length of the span
        for i in range(n - length + 1):  # start of the span
            j = i + length - 1  # end of the span
            for k in range(i, j):  # position to split the span
                for var, productions in grammar.items():
                    for production in productions:
                        if len(production) == 2:  # Only binary
                        ↪   productions in CNF
                            B, C = production
                            if (parse_table[i, k,
                            ↪   variables.index(B)] and
                                parse_table[k + 1, j,
                                ↪   variables.index(C)]):
                                parse_table[i, j,
                                ↪   variables.index(var)] = True

    # Check if the start variable covers the entire string
    start_symbol = 'S'  # Assume 'S' is the start symbol in the
    ↪   grammar
    return parse_table[0, n - 1, variables.index(start_symbol)]

# Example usage
cnf_grammar = {
    'S': [('A', 'B')],
    'A': [('B', 'C'), ('a',)],
    'B': [('b',)],
    'C': [('c',)]
}
input_string = "abc"

result = cyk_algorithm(cnf_grammar, input_string)
print("String can be generated by the grammar:" if result else
↪   "String cannot be generated by the grammar.")
```

This code defines the core functions necessary for parsing strings using the CYK algorithm:

- The `cyk_algorithm` function checks if a given string matches a context-free grammar using a dynamic programming approach.

44

- The grammar is expected to be in Chomsky Normal Form (CNF), represented as a dictionary.

- The input string is parsed by filling a table with possible variable derivations.

- The algorithm then determines if the start symbol of the grammar can be used to generate the entire string.

- The example demonstrates parsing the string "abc" with a given context-free grammar, printing the result.

Chapter 14

Johnson's Algorithm for Sparse Graphs

Below is a Python code snippet that demonstrates the implementation of Johnson's algorithm for finding shortest paths between all pairs of vertices in a sparse, weighted, directed graph using reweighting techniques to handle negative weights.

```python
import heapq

class Graph:
    def __init__(self, vertices):
        self.V = vertices      # Number of vertices
        self.edges = []        # Edges in the graph

    def add_edge(self, u, v, w):
        '''Add an edge from vertex u to v with weight w'''
        self.edges.append((u, v, w))

    def bellman_ford(self, src):
        '''Bellman-Ford algorithm to find shortest paths from src in
        ↪  graphs with negative weight edges'''
        dist = {i: float('Inf') for i in range(self.V)}
        dist[src] = 0

        for _ in range(self.V - 1):
            for u, v, w in self.edges:
                if dist[u] != float('Inf') and dist[u] + w <
                ↪  dist[v]:
                    dist[v] = dist[u] + w

        for u, v, w in self.edges:
            if dist[u] != float('Inf') and dist[u] + w < dist[v]:
```

```
                    raise ValueError("Graph contains negative weight
                    ↪  cycle")

        return dist

    def dijkstra(self, modified_graph, src):
        '''Dijkstra's algorithm to find shortest paths from src'''
        dist = {i: float('Inf') for i in range(self.V)}
        dist[src] = 0
        pq = []
        heapq.heappush(pq, (0, src))

        while pq:
            current_dist, u = heapq.heappop(pq)

            if current_dist > dist[u]:
                continue

            for v, weight in modified_graph[u]:
                distance = current_dist + weight
                if distance < dist[v]:
                    dist[v] = distance
                    heapq.heappush(pq, (distance, v))

        return dist

    def johnson(self):
        '''Johnson's algorithm for all-pairs shortest paths'''
        # Step 1: Add a new vertex and add zero-weight edges to all
        ↪  vertices
        temp_graph = Graph(self.V + 1)
        for (u, v, w) in self.edges:
            temp_graph.add_edge(u, v, w)
        for i in range(self.V):
            temp_graph.add_edge(self.V, i, 0)

        # Step 2: Run Bellman-Ford from the new vertex to calculate
        ↪  h values
        h = temp_graph.bellman_ford(self.V)

        # Step 3: Reweight all edges according to h
        modified_graph = [[] for _ in range(self.V)]
        for u, v, w in self.edges:
            new_weight = w + h[u] - h[v]
            modified_graph[u].append((v, new_weight))

        # Step 4: Run Dijkstra for each vertex
        distances = {}
        for u in range(self.V):
            distances[u] = self.dijkstra(modified_graph, u)

        # Step 5: Adjust the results to remove the effect of h
        for u in range(self.V):
```

```
            for v in range(self.V):
                if distances[u][v] != float('Inf'):
                    distances[u][v] += h[v] - h[u]

        return distances

# Example Usage
graph = Graph(5)
graph.add_edge(0, 1, -1)
graph.add_edge(0, 2, 4)
graph.add_edge(1, 2, 3)
graph.add_edge(1, 3, 2)
graph.add_edge(1, 4, 2)
graph.add_edge(3, 2, 5)
graph.add_edge(3, 1, 1)
graph.add_edge(4, 3, -3)

try:
    all_pairs_shortest_paths = graph.johnson()
    for u in range(graph.V):
        print(f"Distances from vertex {u}:
        ↪ {all_pairs_shortest_paths[u]}")
except ValueError as e:
    print(e)
```

In the implementation above, the function **johnson** performs the following key steps to compute the shortest paths:

- Adding a temporary vertex to facilitate the use of the **bellman_ford** function for reweighting.

- Applying the **bellman_ford** function to calculate potential (h values) to prevent negative weights by reweighting the edges.

- Adjusting the original graph edges using these potential values.

- Using the **dijkstra** function to compute shortest paths from each vertex.

- Correcting the output of **dijkstra** to ensure it matches the original graph weights.

This code is structured to facilitate understanding and ensure that negative weight cycles are properly managed, ensuring reliable path calculations.

Chapter 15

Edmonds-Karp Algorithm for Maximum Flow

Below is a Python code snippet that encompasses the core computational elements of the Edmonds-Karp algorithm for computing the maximum flow in a flow network. This implementation uses the Breadth-First Search (BFS) approach to find augmenting paths and leverages a capacity matrix to manage flow constraints between nodes in the network.

```python
from collections import deque

def bfs(residual_graph, source, sink, parent):
    '''
    Performs Breadth-First Search on the residual graph to find an
    ↪   augmenting path.
    :param residual_graph: 2D list representing capacities of the
    ↪   residual graph.
    :param source: The source node in the flow network.
    :param sink: The sink node in the flow network.
    :param parent: List to store the path from source to sink.
    :return: Boolean indicating the presence of an augmenting path.
    '''
    visited = [False] * len(residual_graph)
    queue = deque([source])
    visited[source] = True

    while queue:
        current_node = queue.popleft()
```

```
            for neighbor, capacity in
            ↪   enumerate(residual_graph[current_node]):
                if not visited[neighbor] and capacity > 0:
                    queue.append(neighbor)
                    visited[neighbor] = True
                    parent[neighbor] = current_node
                    if neighbor == sink:
                        return True

    return False

def edmonds_karp(capacity_matrix, source, sink):
    '''
    Implements the Edmonds-Karp algorithm to compute maximum flow
    ↪   from source to sink.
    :param capacity_matrix: 2D list representing capacities of the
    ↪   flow network.
    :param source: The source node in the flow network.
    :param sink: The sink node in the flow network.
    :return: The total maximum flow possible in the network.
    '''
    num_nodes = len(capacity_matrix)
    residual_graph = [list(row) for row in capacity_matrix]
    parent = [-1] * num_nodes
    max_flow = 0

    while bfs(residual_graph, source, sink, parent):
        path_flow = float('Inf')
        s = sink

        while s != source:
            path_flow = min(path_flow, residual_graph[parent[s]][s])
            s = parent[s]

        max_flow += path_flow

        v = sink
        while v != source:
            u = parent[v]
            residual_graph[u][v] -= path_flow
            residual_graph[v][u] += path_flow
            v = parent[v]

    return max_flow

# Example usage
capacity_matrix = [
    [0, 16, 13, 0, 0, 0],
    [0, 0, 10, 12, 0, 0],
    [0, 4, 0, 0, 14, 0],
    [0, 0, 9, 0, 0, 20],
    [0, 0, 0, 7, 0, 4],
```

```
    [0, 0, 0, 0, 0, 0]
]

source = 0  # Source node
sink = 5  # Sink node

# Calculate maximum flow
max_flow = edmonds_karp(capacity_matrix, source, sink)
print("The maximum possible flow is:", max_flow)
```

This code defines the essential functions required for executing the Edmonds-Karp algorithm within a network flow problem:

- The **bfs** function locates an augmenting path in the residual graph using breadth-first search, updating the **parent** list to reconstruct this path.

- The **edmonds_karp** function iteratively applies BFS to find augmenting paths and updates the flow network and residual capacities, ultimately yielding the maximum flow value.

The example at the end demonstrates an application of the algorithm within a simple network, calculating maximum flow from a given source to a given sink using a capacity matrix. The implementation effectively captures the polynomial complexity of this algorithm in finding augmenting paths, which is crucial for large-scale network flow computations.

Chapter 16

Hopcroft-Karp Algorithm for Maximum Bipartite Matching

Below is a Python code snippet implementing the Hopcroft-Karp algorithm for finding maximum cardinality matchings in bipartite graphs, using BFS and DFS to discover augmenting paths.

```python
from collections import deque

def bfs(pair_u, pair_v, dist, u_nodes, v_nodes, adj_list):
    queue = deque()
    for u in u_nodes:
        if pair_u[u] == None:
            dist[u] = 0
            queue.append(u)
        else:
            dist[u] = float('inf')
    dist[None] = float('inf')

    while queue:
        u = queue.popleft()
        if dist[u] < dist[None]:
            for v in adj_list[u]:
                if dist[pair_v[v]] == float('inf'):
                    dist[pair_v[v]] = dist[u] + 1
                    queue.append(pair_v[v])
    return dist[None] != float('inf')
```

```
def dfs(u, pair_u, pair_v, dist, adj_list):
    if u is not None:
        for v in adj_list[u]:
            if dist[pair_v[v]] == dist[u] + 1:
                if dfs(pair_v[v], pair_u, pair_v, dist, adj_list):
                    pair_v[v] = u
                    pair_u[u] = v
                    return True
        dist[u] = float('inf')
        return False
    return True

def hopcroft_karp(u_nodes, v_nodes, adj_list):
    pair_u = {u: None for u in u_nodes}
    pair_v = {v: None for v in v_nodes}
    dist = {}

    matching = 0
    while bfs(pair_u, pair_v, dist, u_nodes, v_nodes, adj_list):
        for u in u_nodes:
            if pair_u[u] is None:
                if dfs(u, pair_u, pair_v, dist, adj_list):
                    matching += 1
    return matching

# Example graph
u_nodes = {1, 2, 3, 4}
v_nodes = {5, 6, 7, 8}
adj_list = {
    1: [5, 6],
    2: [5],
    3: [6, 7],
    4: [7, 8]
}

result = hopcroft_karp(u_nodes, v_nodes, adj_list)
print("Maximum Matching:", result)
```

This code defines key components for implementing the Hopcroft-Karp algorithm to find a maximum matching:

- The bfs function performs a Breadth-First Search to calculate distances and prepare matched and unmatched vertices.

- The dfs function performs a Depth-First Search to explore augmenting paths and update matching pairs.

- The hopcroft_karp function coordinates the BFS and DFS calls to find the maximum cardinality matching in a bipartite graph.

- The sample graph is constructed with nodes divided into two partitions, `u_nodes` and `v_nodes`, connected by an adjacency list `adj_list`.

- The result is printed as the maximum number of matching pairs found.

Chapter 17

Tarjan's Strongly Connected Components Algorithm

Below is a Python code snippet that encompasses the core computational elements of Tarjan's algorithm for identifying strongly connected components, including the use of depth-first search and low-link values to efficiently find all strongly connected components in a directed graph.

```python
class Graph:
    def __init__(self, vertices):
        self.vertices = vertices   # Number of vertices in the graph
        self.graph = {}   # Adjacency list representation of the
        ↪ graph
        self.time = 0   # Time counter for DFS

    def add_edge(self, u, v):
        if u in self.graph:
            self.graph[u].append(v)
        else:
            self.graph[u] = [v]

    def _strongconnect(self, v, low, num, stack, on_stack, sccs):
        # Initializing discovery time and low value of vertex v
        num[v] = low[v] = self.time
        self.time += 1
        stack.append(v)
        on_stack[v] = True
```

```python
        # Consider successors of v
        for w in self.graph.get(v, []):
            if num[w] == -1:  # w has not been visited
                self._strongconnect(w, low, num, stack, on_stack,
                ↪   sccs)
                low[v] = min(low[v], low[w])
            elif on_stack[w]:
                low[v] = min(low[v], num[w])

        # If v is a root node, pop the stack and form an SCC
        if low[v] == num[v]:
            current_scc = []
            while True:
                w = stack.pop()
                on_stack[w] = False
                current_scc.append(w)
                if w == v:
                    break
            sccs.append(current_scc)

    def find_sccs(self):
        num = {v: -1 for v in range(self.vertices)}  # To track
        ↪   discovery times of visited vertices
        low = {v: -1 for v in range(self.vertices)}  # To store the
        ↪   earliest visited vertex reachable from a vertex
        on_stack = [False] * self.vertices  # Bookkeeping for stack
        ↪   inclusion
        stack = []  # To store the vertices on the current search
        ↪   path
        sccs = []  # To record all strongly connected components

        # Call the recursive helper function to find SCCs
        for v in range(self.vertices):
            if num[v] == -1:
                self._strongconnect(v, low, num, stack, on_stack,
                ↪   sccs)

        return sccs

# Create a graph given in the above diagrams
g = Graph(5)
g.add_edge(1, 0)
g.add_edge(0, 2)
g.add_edge(2, 1)
g.add_edge(0, 3)
g.add_edge(3, 4)

sccs = g.find_sccs()  # Get the strongly connected components
print("Strongly Connected Components:", sccs)
```

This code defines several key functions necessary for the implementation of Tarjan's algorithm for identifying strongly connected components in a directed graph:

- The `Graph` class manages graph representation and operations.

- `add_edge` method adds directed edges between vertices.

- The `_strongconnect` function is a recursive helper that applies a depth-first search to calculate discovery and low-link values, identifying SCCs when a root node (vertex with no back-edge parent) is reached.

- `find_sccs` invokes Tarjan's SCC algorithm for all vertices, returning a list of SCCs in the graph.

The final block demonstrates constructing a graph, applying the SCC search, and printing the found components.

Chapter 18

Kosaraju's Algorithm for Strong Connectivity

Below is a Python code snippet that implements Kosaraju's algorithm for finding strongly connected components (SCCs) in a directed graph. The implementation details the use of two-pass depth-first search (DFS) for component discovery and utilizes adjacency list representation for the graph.

```python
from collections import defaultdict

def kosaraju_scc(n, edges):
    '''
    Kosaraju's algorithm to find strongly connected components.
    :param n: Number of vertices in the graph.
    :param edges: Directed edges of the graph as pairs (u, v).
    :return: List of strongly connected components.
    '''
    def dfs_first_pass(v, visited, stack):
        visited[v] = True
        for u in transpose_graph[v]:
            if not visited[u]:
                dfs_first_pass(u, visited, stack)
        stack.append(v)

    def dfs_second_pass(v, visited, current_scc):
        visited[v] = True
        current_scc.append(v)
        for u in original_graph[v]:
            if not visited[u]:
                dfs_second_pass(u, visited, current_scc)
```

```python
# Step 1: Initialize graphs
original_graph = defaultdict(list)
transpose_graph = defaultdict(list)

for u, v in edges:
    original_graph[u].append(v)
    transpose_graph[v].append(u)

# Step 2: First DFS to order vertices
visited = [False] * n
finish_stack = []

for i in range(n):
    if not visited[i]:
        dfs_first_pass(i, visited, finish_stack)

# Step 3: Second DFS on transposed graph using the finish order
visited = [False] * n
sccs = []

while finish_stack:
    v = finish_stack.pop()
    if not visited[v]:
        current_scc = []
        dfs_second_pass(v, visited, current_scc)
        sccs.append(current_scc)

return sccs

# Sample usage:
# Graph: 0 -> 1, 1 -> 2, 2 -> 0, 2 -> 3, 3 -> 4
edges = [(0, 1), (1, 2), (2, 0), (2, 3), (3, 4)]
n = 5 # Number of vertices in the graph
sccs = kosaraju_scc(n, edges)
print("Strongly Connected Components:", sccs)
```

This code provides an implementation of Kosaraju's algorithm with the following key functions:

- The graph input is handled using an adjacency list for both the original and transposed graphs.

- The `dfs_first_pass` function conducts the first DFS on the transposed graph to determine vertex finish order.

- The `dfs_second_pass` function executes the second DFS on the original graph, utilizing the finish order to discover SCCs.

- Finally, the `kosaraju_scc` function manages the graph processing and returns the list of strongly connected components.

By leveraging Kosaraju's algorithm, this implementation efficiently finds all SCCs by conducting two DFS traversals, ensuring each component is identified correctly.

Chapter 19

Miller-Rabin Probabilistic Primality Test

Below is a Python code snippet that provides an implementation of the Miller-Rabin probabilistic primality testing algorithm, including functions for witness selection and estimation of error probability in primality assessment.

```python
import random

def miller_rabin_test(n, k):
    '''
    Perform the Miller-Rabin primality test on an integer n using k
    ↪ iterations.
    :param n: The integer to test for primality.
    :param k: Number of iterations to perform.
    :return: True if n is likely prime, False if composite.
    '''
    # Trivial cases
    if n <= 1:
        return False
    if n <= 3:
        return True
    if n % 2 == 0:
        return False

    # Decompose (n-1) as 2^s * d
    s, d = 0, n - 1
    while d % 2 == 0:
        s += 1
```

```
            d //= 2

    def is_composite(a, s, d, n):
        # Check if a is a composite witness for n
        x = pow(a, d, n)
        if x == 1 or x == n - 1:
            return False
        for _ in range(s - 1):
            x = pow(x, 2, n)
            if x == n - 1:
                return False
        return True

    # Perform k rounds of testing
    for _ in range(k):
        a = random.randrange(2, n - 1)
        if is_composite(a, s, d, n):
            return False

    return True

def select_witnesses(n, k):
    '''
    Select and test a number of witnesses for the primality of n.
    :param n: The integer to test for primality.
    :param k: Number of witnesses to potentially select.
    :return: List of witnesses where n is probable non-prime.
    '''
    witnesses = []
    for _ in range(k):
        a = random.randrange(2, n - 1)
        if not miller_rabin_test(n, 1):
            witnesses.append(a)
    return witnesses

def calculate_error_probability(k):
    '''
    Calculate the error probability for the Miller-Rabin test given
    ↪ k iterations.
    :param k: Number of iterations performed.
    :return: Upper bound on the probability of error.
    '''
    return 1 / (4 ** k)

# Example Usage
n = 561   # Known Carmichael number
k = 5     # Number of iterations
is_prime = miller_rabin_test(n, k)
witnesses = select_witnesses(n, k)
error_prob = calculate_error_probability(k)

print("Is Prime:", is_prime)
print("Witnesses (if any):", witnesses)
```

```
print("Error Probability:", error_prob)
```

This code provides essential functions for performing the Miller-Rabin probabilistic primality test:

- `miller_rabin_test` checks if a number is likely prime by executing multiple rounds with different random bases.

- `select_witnesses` identifies and tests potential witnesses for composite numbers.

- `calculate_error_probability` computes the probability of incorrectly classifying a composite number as prime after a given number of iterations.

The final section demonstrates testing a known Carmichael number with specified iterations and evaluates the error probability.

Chapter 20

Monte Carlo Algorithms and Randomization Techniques

Below is a Python code snippet that demonstrates the application of Monte Carlo algorithms for the estimation of the value of through the technique of numerical integration using random sampling.

```python
import numpy as np

def monte_carlo_pi(num_points):
    '''
    Estimate the value of  using the Monte Carlo method.
    :param num_points: The number of random points to generate.
    :return: The estimated value of .
    '''
    inside_circle = 0

    for _ in range(num_points):
        x, y = np.random.uniform(-1, 1, 2)  # Generate random point
        ↪  (x, y)
        if x**2 + y**2 <= 1:
            inside_circle += 1  # Point is inside the circle

    return (inside_circle / num_points) * 4
```

```
# Example usage
estimated_pi = monte_carlo_pi(10000)
print("Estimated value of :", estimated_pi)
```

This Python code snippet includes the core computational elements for using the Monte Carlo method to estimate the value of π through random sampling:

- `monte_carlo_pi` function: This function generates a specified number of random points and determines the proportion of these that fall within a unit circle. It uses this proportion to estimate π.

The final block demonstrates the execution of the Monte Carlo method by estimating π with a sample size of 10,000 points.

Chapter 21

Las Vegas Algorithms: Zero-Error Randomized Algorithms

Below is a Python code snippet that illustrates the implementation of a Las Vegas type algorithm using randomized quicksort. This approach ensures that the sorting is always accurate while allowing for probabilistic runtime efficiency.

```python
import random

def randomized_quick_sort(arr):
    '''
    Performs a randomized quicksort on the given list.
    :param arr: List of elements to be sorted.
    :return: Sorted list.
    '''
    if len(arr) <= 1:
        return arr
    else:
        pivot_index = random.randint(0, len(arr) - 1)
        pivot = arr[pivot_index]
        less_than_pivot = [x for i, x in enumerate(arr) if x <=
        ↪   pivot and i != pivot_index]
        greater_than_pivot = [x for x in arr if x > pivot]
        return randomized_quick_sort(less_than_pivot) + [pivot] +
        ↪   randomized_quick_sort(greater_than_pivot)
```

```
# Example usage:
unsorted_array = [3, 6, 8, 10, 1, 2, 1]
print("Unsorted array:", unsorted_array)
sorted_array = randomized_quick_sort(unsorted_array)
print("Sorted array:", sorted_array)
```

This code snippet details the process of implementing a randomized version of the quicksort algorithm:

- `randomized_quick_sort` function recursively sorts an array by selecting a random pivot.

- The use of a random pivot helps in achieving the average-case time complexity more reliably, countering worst-case scenarios typically encountered in standard quicksorts.

- `less_than_pivot` and `greater_than_pivot` lists are used to partition the array around the randomly chosen pivot.

- The function guarantees convergence to a correctly sorted list while taking advantage of randomized runtimes for efficiency.

This implementation demonstrates how randomness can be effectively employed to maintain the correctness of an algorithm while optimizing performance.

Chapter 22

Skip Lists: Probabilistic Data Structures

Below is a Python code snippet that encompasses the core operations of a skip list including insertion, deletion, and search, all achieving expected logarithmic time complexity through probabilistic balancing.

```python
import random

class Node:
    def __init__(self, key, level):
        self.key = key
        self.forward = [None] * (level + 1)

class SkipList:
    def __init__(self, max_lvl, p):
        self.MAXLVL = max_lvl
        self.p = p
        self.header = self._create_node(self.MAXLVL, -1)
        self.level = 0

    def _create_node(self, lvl, key):
        return Node(key, lvl)

    def _random_level(self):
        lvl = 0
        while random.random() < self.p and lvl < self.MAXLVL:
            lvl += 1
        return lvl
```

```python
def insert_element(self, key):
    update = [None] * (self.MAXLVL + 1)
    current = self.header

    for i in range(self.level, -1, -1):
        while current.forward[i] and current.forward[i].key <
        ↪  key:
            current = current.forward[i]
        update[i] = current

    current = current.forward[0]

    if current is None or current.key != key:
        rand_lvl = self._random_level()

        if rand_lvl > self.level:
            for i in range(self.level + 1, rand_lvl + 1):
                update[i] = self.header
            self.level = rand_lvl

        new_node = self._create_node(rand_lvl, key)
        for i in range(rand_lvl + 1):
            new_node.forward[i] = update[i].forward[i]
            update[i].forward[i] = new_node

def delete_element(self, key):
    update = [None] * (self.MAXLVL + 1)
    current = self.header

    for i in range(self.level, -1, -1):
        while current.forward[i] and current.forward[i].key <
        ↪  key:
            current = current.forward[i]
        update[i] = current

    current = current.forward[0]

    if current is not None and current.key == key:
        for i in range(self.level + 1):
            if update[i].forward[i] != current:
                break
            update[i].forward[i] = current.forward[i]

        while self.level > 0 and self.header.forward[self.level]
        ↪  is None:
            self.level -= 1

def search_element(self, key):
    current = self.header
    for i in range(self.level, -1, -1):
        while current.forward[i] and current.forward[i].key <
        ↪  key:
```

```
                    current = current.forward[i]

            current = current.forward[0]

            if current and current.key == key:
                return True
            return False

# Example usage
skip_list = SkipList(3, 0.5)
skip_list.insert_element(3)
skip_list.insert_element(6)
skip_list.insert_element(7)
skip_list.insert_element(9)
skip_list.insert_element(12)

print("Search 9:", skip_list.search_element(9))
print("Search 15:", skip_list.search_element(15))

skip_list.delete_element(9)
print("Search 9 after deletion:", skip_list.search_element(9))
```

This code defines the necessary components and functions for implementing skip lists:

- **Node** class captures the structure of each skip list node with pointers for various levels.

- **SkipList** class orchestrates the skip list operations with methods for node creation, random level determination, insertion, deletion, and search.

- **insert_element** adds elements to the skip list, adjusting pointers and levels to maintain expected logarithmic performance.

- **delete_element** removes a specified element, updating level adjustments as needed.

- **search_element** checks for the presence of a key, leveraging the skip list's multiple level pointers for efficiency.

The example usage demonstrates insertion, search, and deletion within the skip list structure.

Chapter 23

Graham's Scan Algorithm for Convex Hulls

Below is a Python code snippet that demonstrates the implementation of Graham's Scan algorithm for computing the convex hull of a set of points in the plane. The algorithm sorts the points by polar angle and uses a stack-based approach to construct the hull.

```python
import math

# Function to calculate the orientation of the ordered triplet (p,
↪    q, r).
def orientation(p, q, r):
    '''
    Return 0 if p, q and r are collinear, 1 if Clockwise, 2 if
    ↪    Counterclockwise
    '''
    val = (q[1] - p[1]) * (r[0] - q[0]) - (q[0] - p[0]) * (r[1] -
    ↪    q[1])
    if val == 0:
        return 0
    elif val > 0:
        return 1
    else:
        return 2

# Function to determine the square of the Euclidean distance between
↪    two points
def distance_squared(p, q):
    return (q[0] - p[0]) ** 2 + (q[1] - p[1]) ** 2
```

```python
# Function to find the convex hull using Graham's Scan algorithm
def graham_scan(points):
    '''
    Computes the convex hull of a set of 2D points.
    :param points: List of (x, y) tuples representing the points.
    :return: List of vertices representing the convex hull in
    ↪    counterclockwise order
    '''
    N = len(points)
    if N < 3:
        return None

    # Find the bottom-most point (or choose the left most point in
    ↪    case of tie)
    min_y_index = 0
    for i in range(1, N):
        if points[i][1] < points[min_y_index][1] or (
            points[i][1] == points[min_y_index][1] and points[i][0] <
            ↪    points[min_y_index][0]):
            min_y_index = i

    # Place the bottom-most point at first position
    points[0], points[min_y_index] = points[min_y_index], points[0]

    # Sort the points based on the polar angle with the first point
    base_point = points[0]
    sorted_points = sorted(points[1:], key=lambda p:
    ↪    (math.atan2(p[1] - base_point[1],
                      p[0] - base_point[0]),
                -distance_squared(base_point, p)))

    # Add the first point at the end to loop back
    sorted_points.append(points[0])

    # Initialize a stack and push first three points to it
    stack = [points[0], sorted_points[0], sorted_points[1]]

    # Process the remaining points
    for i in range(2, len(sorted_points)):
        while len(stack) > 1 and orientation(stack[-2], stack[-1],
        ↪    sorted_points[i]) != 2:
            stack.pop()
        stack.append(sorted_points[i])

    return stack[:-1]    # Return the result without adding the first
    ↪    point

# Example usage:
points = [(0, 0), (1, 1), (2, 2), (4, 4), (0, 4), (4, 0), (1, 2),
↪    (2, 1), (3, 3), (3, 0)]
convex_hull = graham_scan(points)
```

```
print("Convex Hull:", convex_hull)
```

The code defines the essential components required for Graham's Scan algorithm to compute the convex hull:

- **orientation**: This function helps determine the orientation of three points, needed to decide if a point should be part of the hull.

- **distance_squared**: Calculates the squared distance between two points, helping in sorting operations.

- **graham_scan**: Implements the Graham's Scan algorithm, leveraging a stack-based mechanism to construct the convex hull by processing the sorted list of points.

The code includes a sample dataset through the **points** list, and upon execution, identifies and prints the vertices forming the convex hull in counterclockwise order.

Chapter 24

Jarvis March Algorithm for Convex Hulls

Below is a Python code snippet that encapsulates the Jarvis March, or Gift Wrapping algorithm, for convex hull computation. The code identifies the convex hull points by performing angular scanning.

```python
import numpy as np

def orientation(p, q, r):
    '''
    Determine the orientation of the triplet (p, q, r).
    :param p: First point.
    :param q: Second point.
    :param r: Third point.
    :return: 0 if collinear, 1 if clockwise, 2 if counterclockwise.
    '''
    val = (q[1] - p[1]) * (r[0] - q[0]) - (q[0] - p[0]) * (r[1] -
    ↪    q[1])
    if val == 0:
        return 0
    elif val > 0:
        return 1
    else:
        return 2

def jarvis_march(points):
    '''
    Performs the Jarvis March algorithm to find the convex hull of a
    ↪    set of 2D points.
```

```
    :param points: List of points (tuples).
    :return: Convex hull points in counter-clockwise order.
    '''
    n = len(points)
    if n < 3:
        return points

    hull = []

    # Find the leftmost point
    leftmost = 0
    for i in range(1, n):
        if points[i][0] < points[leftmost][0]:
            leftmost = i

    p = leftmost
    while True:
        # Add current point to hull
        hull.append(points[p])

        # Search for the next point in the hull
        q = (p + 1) % n
        for i in range(n):
            if orientation(points[p], points[i], points[q]) == 2:
                q = i

        # Update p to q
        p = q

        # Break the loop if returned to the start
        if p == leftmost:
            break

    return hull

# Example usage
points = [(0, 0), (1, 1), (2, 2), (3, 0), (2, 1), (1, 3)]
hull_points = jarvis_march(points)
print("The points in the convex hull are:", hull_points)
```

This code defines important functions necessary for executing the Jarvis March algorithm:

- **orientation** function computes the orientation of three ordered points (collinear, clockwise, counterclockwise).

- **jarvis_march** identifies and returns the set of points making up the convex hull in counterclockwise order.

- The final block demonstrates usage, computing the convex hull for a provided set of 2D points.

The algorithm iteratively wraps points into the hull by selecting the most counter-clockwise point from the current point.

Chapter 25

Quickhull Algorithm for Convex Hulls

Below is a Python code snippet that implements the Quickhull algorithm for computing the convex hull of a set of points. It exploits principles of the quicksort algorithm and employs divide-and-conquer strategies to achieve efficient convex hull computation.

```python
import numpy as np

def quickhull(points):
    """
    Compute the convex hull of a set of 2D points using the
    ↪ Quickhull algorithm.
    :param points: List or numpy array of points (x, y).
    :return: The convex hull as a list of points.
    """
    # Find the points with min and max x-coordinates, these are
    ↪ definitely part of the hull
    points = sorted(points, key=lambda x: x[0])
    leftmost = points[0]
    rightmost = points[-1]

    # Split the remaining points into two groups: above and below
    ↪ the line formed by the leftmost and rightmost
    above = []
    below = []
    for p in points[1:-1]:
        if _is_above_line(leftmost, rightmost, p):
            above.append(p)
        else:
            below.append(p)
```

```python
    # Find hull points across the line AB and BA
    hull = [leftmost] + _find_hull(above, leftmost, rightmost) +
    ↪   [rightmost] + _find_hull(below, rightmost, leftmost)
    return hull

def _distance(p1, p2, p):
    """
    Calculate the signed distance from point p to the line defined
    ↪   by points p1 and p2.
    :param p1: First point on the line.
    :param p2: Second point on the line.
    :param p: Point for which distance is to be calculated.
    :return: Signed distance from p to the line.
    """
    return (p[1] - p1[1]) * (p2[0] - p1[0]) - (p[0] - p1[0]) *
    ↪   (p2[1] - p1[1])

def _is_above_line(p1, p2, p):
    """
    Determine if point p is above the line formed by points p1 and
    ↪   p2.
    :param p1: First point on the line.
    :param p2: Second point on the line.
    :param p: Point to test.
    :return: True if p is above the line, False otherwise.
    """
    return _distance(p1, p2, p) > 0

def _find_hull(points, p1, p2):
    """
    Find the subset of points that form the convex hull between p1
    ↪   and p2.
    :param points: List of points.
    :param p1: Starting point of the line.
    :param p2: Ending point of the line.
    :return: The convex hull points between p1 and p2.
    """
    if not points:
        return []

    # Find the point 'p' with maximum distance from line segment
    ↪   (p1, p2)
    p = max(points, key=lambda x: _distance(p1, p2, x))

    # Filter points that are strictly outside the triangle formed by
    ↪   p1, p, p2
    points_left_of_line = [x for x in points if _distance(p1, p, x)
    ↪   > 0]
    points_right_of_line = [x for x in points if _distance(p, p2, x)
    ↪   > 0]

    # Recursively find further points on the convex hull to the left
    ↪   and right of the line segments
```

```
    return _find_hull(points_left_of_line, p1, p) + [p] +
    ↪   _find_hull(points_right_of_line, p, p2)

# Example usage with a set of random points
np.random.seed(0)
points = np.random.rand(10, 2)
convex_hull = quickhull(points)

print("Points in Convex Hull:", convex_hull)
```

This code defines several key functions necessary for computing
the convex hull using the Quickhull algorithm:

- `quickhull` is the main function that initializes and drives the
  convex hull computation.

- `_distance` computes the signed distance of a point from a
  line defined by two points.

- `_is_above_line` determines if a point lies above the line
  formed by two other points.

- `_find_hull` recursively finds the points that form the convex hull between two endpoints by evaluating distances and
  filtering.

The final block demonstrates how the `quickhull` function can
be used with a sample set of random points to compute their convex
hull.

Chapter 26

Delaunay Triangulation and Computational Geometry

Below is a Python code snippet that demonstrates the construction of a Delaunay Triangulation and its relationship with Voronoi diagrams using computational geometry principles.

```python
import numpy as np
from scipy.spatial import Delaunay, Voronoi, voronoi_plot_2d
import matplotlib.pyplot as plt

def generate_points(n_points, seed=None):
    '''
    Generates random points for triangulation and Voronoi diagram
    ↪   construction.
    :param n_points: Number of points to generate.
    :param seed: Seed for the random number generator for
    ↪   reproducibility.
    :return: Array of points.
    '''
    np.random.seed(seed)
    points = np.random.rand(n_points, 2)    # Random points in 2D
    return points

def delaunay_triangulation(points):
    '''
    Performs Delaunay triangulation on a set of points.
    :param points: Array of points for triangulation.
    :return: Delaunay triangulation object.
    '''
```

```
    tri = Delaunay(points)
    return tri

def plot_delaunay(tri, points):
    '''
    Plots the Delaunay triangulation and its circumcircles.
    :param tri: Delaunay triangulation object.
    :param points: Array of points used for triangulation.
    '''
    plt.triplot(points[:, 0], points[:, 1], tri.simplices)
    plt.plot(points[:, 0], points[:, 1], 'o')
    plt.title('Delaunay Triangulation')
    plt.show()

def voronoi_diagram(points):
    '''
    Creates and plots the Voronoi diagram from a set of points.
    :param points: Array of points for Voronoi diagram.
    '''
    vor = Voronoi(points)
    voronoi_plot_2d(vor)
    plt.plot(points[:, 0], points[:, 1], 'o')
    plt.title('Voronoi Diagram')
    plt.show()

# Parameters
n = 30   # Number of points
seed = 42   # Seed for reproducibility

# Generate random points
points = generate_points(n, seed)

# Perform Delaunay triangulation
tri = delaunay_triangulation(points)

# Plot Delaunay triangulation
plot_delaunay(tri, points)

# Generate and plot Voronoi diagram for the same set of points
voronoi_diagram(points)
```

This code snippet highlights the following key computational operations:

- **generate_points**: A function to generate a specified number of 2D points using NumPy for randomness, crucial for any geometric computation requiring random sampling.

- **delaunay_triangulation**: Constructs a Delaunay triangulation using the SciPy **Delaunay** class, which provides connectivity information defining the triangular faces.

- `plot_delaunay`: Utilizes Matplotlib to visualize the computed Delaunay triangles, offering insights into how points are interconnected.

- `voronoi_diagram`: Constructs the Voronoi diagram linked to the Delaunay triangulation, using `Voronoi` and `voronoi_plot_2d` from SciPy for visualization, highlighting the dual nature of these geometric constructs.

Both the Delaunay Triangulation and Voronoi Diagram are core concepts in computational geometry with widespread applications in graphics, spatial data analysis, and scientific computing.

Chapter 27

Voronoi Diagrams and Nearest Neighbor Queries

Below is a Python code snippet that encompasses the core computational elements of constructing Voronoi diagrams using Fortune's
algorithm, which efficiently computes the diagram by incrementally
processing each site and maintaining a beach line.

```python
import heapq
import itertools
from collections import defaultdict
import matplotlib.pyplot as plt
import numpy as np

class Event:
    def __init__(self, x, point, arc=None):
        self.x = x
        self.point = point
        self.arc = arc
        self.valid = True

class Arc:
    def __init__(self, point):
        self.point = point
        self.prev = None
        self.next = None
        self.event = None
        self.seg1 = None
        self.seg2 = None
```

```python
class Segment:
    def __init__(self, start):
        self.start = start
        self.end = None
        self.done = False

    def finish(self, end):
        if self.done:
            return
        self.end = end
        self.done = True

class Voronoi:
    def __init__(self, points):
        self.points = points
        self.edges = []
        self.result = []

        self.events = []
        self.arcs = None

        self.x0 = 0
        self.x1 = 0
        self.y0 = 0
        self.y1 = 0

        for p in points:
            heapq.heappush(self.events, Event(p[0], p))

    def process(self):
        while self.events:
            event = heapq.heappop(self.events)
            if event.valid:
                if event.arc is not None:
                    self.remove_parabola(event)
                else:
                    self.add_parabola(event.point)

    def add_parabola(self, point):
        if self.arcs is None:
            self.arcs = Arc(point)
            return

        arc = self.arcs
        while arc is not None:
            intersection, cx, cy = self.intersect(point, arc)
            if intersection:
                break
            arc = arc.next

        if arc.event is not None:
            arc.event.valid = False
        new_arc1 = Arc(arc.point)
```

```python
        new_arc2 = Arc(point)
        new_arc3 = Arc(arc.point)

        new_arc1.next = new_arc2
        new_arc2.prev = new_arc1
        new_arc2.next = new_arc3
        new_arc3.prev = new_arc2

        if arc.prev is not None:
            arc.prev.next = new_arc1
        new_arc1.prev = arc.prev
        if arc.next is not None:
            arc.next.prev = new_arc3
        new_arc3.next = arc.next

        if arc == self.arcs:
            self.arcs = new_arc1

        self.check_circle_event(new_arc1)
        self.check_circle_event(new_arc3)

        seg = Segment((cx, cy))
        self.edges.append(seg)
        new_arc2.seg1 = seg
        new_arc3.seg2 = seg

    def remove_parabola(self, event):
        arc = event.arc

        if arc.prev is not None:
            arc.prev.next = arc.next
        if arc.next is not None:
            arc.next.prev = arc.prev

        if arc.seg1 is not None:
            arc.seg1.finish(event.point)
        if arc.seg2 is not None:
            arc.seg2.finish(event.point)

        if arc.prev is not None:
            self.check_circle_event(arc.prev)
        if arc.next is not None:
            self.check_circle_event(arc.next)

    def check_circle_event(self, arc):
        if arc.prev is None or arc.next is None:
            return

        check, x, center = self.circle(arc.prev.point, arc.point,
        ↪   arc.next.point)

        if check:
            event = Event(x, center, arc)
```

```python
            arc.event = event
            heapq.heappush(self.events, event)

    def intersect(self, point, arc):
        if arc.point[0] == point[0]:
            return False, None, None

        a = 2 * (arc.point[0] - point[0])
        b = arc.point[1]**2 - point[1]**2 + point[0]**2 -
        ↪   arc.point[0]**2
        c = point[0] - arc.point[0]

        z = (-b - np.sqrt(b**2 - 4*a*c)) / (2*a)
        bx = (point[0] + arc.point[0]) / 2
        by = (point[1] + arc.point[1]) / 2

        return True, bx, z

    def circle(self, a, b, c):
        if (b[0] - a[0]) * (c[1] - a[1]) - (c[0] - a[0]) * (b[1] -
        ↪   a[1]) > 0:
            return False, None, None

        A = np.array([[2 * (b[0] - a[0]), 2 * (b[1] - a[1])],
                      [2 * (c[0] - a[0]), 2 * (c[1] - a[1])]])
        B = np.array([b[0]**2 - a[0]**2 + b[1]**2 - a[1]**2,
                      c[0]**2 - a[0]**2 + c[1]**2 - a[1]**2])
        center = np.linalg.solve(A, B)

        radius = np.linalg.norm(a - center)
        return True, center[0] + radius, (center[0], center[1])

    def plot(self):
        fig, ax = plt.subplots()
        for seg in self.edges:
            plt.plot([seg.start[0], seg.end[0]], [seg.start[1],
            ↪   seg.end[1]], 'k-')
        ax.set_xlim((self.x0, self.x1))
        ax.set_ylim((self.y0, self.y1))
        plt.show()

# Sample usage
points = np.random.rand(10, 2)
v = Voronoi(points)
v.process()
v.plot()
```

This code defines several core components required for constructing Voronoi diagrams using Fortune's algorithm:

- **Event** and **Arc** classes represent the key elements in maintaining the beach line and processing events.

- **Segment** class is used to store edges of the Voronoi diagram.

- **Voronoi** class houses the main algorithm which involves event processing, adding and removing parabolas, and handling circle events.

- The **process** function manages the main loop for the algorithm, adding sites and removing arcs efficiently.

- **add_parabola** and **remove_parabola** functions handle the dynamic updating of the beach line.

- **check_circle_event** checks for potential circle events which are key to updating the Voronoi edges correctly.

This implementation provides a robust foundation for exploring computational geometry and efficient nearest neighbor queries through the Voronoi structure.

Chapter 28

Bentley-Ottmann Algorithm for Line Segment Intersection

Below is a Python code snippet that implements the Bentley-Ottmann algorithm to report all intersections among a set of line segments using the concepts of event queues and sweep lines.

```python
from sortedcontainers import SortedDict
from collections import namedtuple

Point = namedtuple('Point', ('x', 'y'))
Event = namedtuple('Event', ('point', 'left', 'segment'))

def intersect(s1, s2):
    '''
    Detect if two line segments intersect.
    :param s1: First line segment as a tuple of points (p1, p2).
    :param s2: Second line segment as a tuple of points (p3, p4).
    :return: Boolean indicating if the segments intersect.
    '''
    def ccw(A, B, C):
        return (C.y - A.y) * (B.x - A.x) > (B.y - A.y) * (C.x - A.x)

    p1, p2 = s1
    p3, p4 = s2
    return ccw(p1, p3, p4) != ccw(p2, p3, p4) and ccw(p1, p2, p3) !=
    ↪   ccw(p1, p2, p4)

def bentley_ottmann(segments):
    '''
```

```python
    Implements the Bentley-Ottmann algorithm for finding all
    ↪   intersections.
    :param segments: List of line segments, each represented as a
    ↪   tuple (Point, Point).
    :return: List of intersection points.
    '''
    events = SortedDict()
    status = SortedDict()
    intersections = []

    def add_event(event_point, segment, left):
        event = Event(event_point, left, segment)
        if event_point not in events:
            events[event_point] = []
        events[event_point].append(event)

    for segment in segments:
        p1, p2 = sorted(segment)
        add_event(p1, segment, True)
        add_event(p2, segment, False)

    while events:
        point, current_events = events.popitem(0)

        for event in current_events:
            if event.left:
                status[(event.segment, 'left')] = point
                seg_idx = list(status.keys()).index((event.segment,
                ↪   'left'))
                if seg_idx > 0:
                    pre_seg = list(status.keys())[seg_idx - 1][0]
                    if intersect(pre_seg, event.segment):
                        intersections.append(point)
                if seg_idx + 1 < len(status):
                    next_seg = list(status.keys())[seg_idx + 1][0]
                    if intersect(event.segment, next_seg):
                        intersections.append(point)
            else:
                seg_idx = list(status.keys()).index((event.segment,
                ↪   'left'))
                if 0 < seg_idx < len(status) - 1:
                    pre_seg = list(status.keys())[seg_idx - 1][0]
                    next_seg = list(status.keys())[seg_idx + 1][0]
                    if intersect(pre_seg, next_seg):
                        intersections.append(point)
                status.pop((event.segment, 'left'))

    return intersections

# Example usage
segments = [
    (Point(0, 0), Point(3, 3)),
    (Point(0, 3), Point(3, 0)),
```

89

```
    (Point(1, 0), Point(1, 3)),
    (Point(0, 2), Point(3, 2))
]

intersections = bentley_ottmann(segments)
print("Intersections:", intersections)
```

This code clearly demonstrates foundational principles of the Bentley-Ottmann algorithm:

- A `Point` and `Event` data structure to manage segments endpoints and events with respect to the sweep line.

- The `intersect` function, crucial for determining the intersection between two segments.

- The core `bentley_ottmann` function manages the event queue using a sorted dictionary and evaluates segment intersections, storing discovered intersections.

An example usage is provided where multiple segments are processed to find intersection points, validating the algorithm's correctness and efficiency.

Chapter 29

Huffman Coding for Data Compression

Below is a Python code snippet that encompasses the core computational elements of Huffman coding, including the construction of Huffman trees and encoding/decoding processes.

```python
import heapq
from collections import defaultdict, Counter

# Node class for building the Huffman tree
class HuffmanNode:
    def __init__(self, char, freq):
        self.char = char
        self.freq = freq
        self.left = None
        self.right = None

    # Override the less than operator for priority queue
    def __lt__(self, other):
        return self.freq < other.freq

def build_huffman_tree(text):
    '''
    Constructs a Huffman tree for the given text.
    :param text: The input string for which to build the tree.
    :return: Root node of the Huffman tree.
    '''

    if not text:
        return None

    frequency = Counter(text)
```

```python
    priority_queue = [HuffmanNode(char, freq) for char, freq in
    ↪  frequency.items()]
    heapq.heapify(priority_queue)

    while len(priority_queue) > 1:
        node1 = heapq.heappop(priority_queue)
        node2 = heapq.heappop(priority_queue)
        merged = HuffmanNode(None, node1.freq + node2.freq)
        merged.left = node1
        merged.right = node2
        heapq.heappush(priority_queue, merged)

    return priority_queue[0] if priority_queue else None

def generate_codes(node, prefix='', codebook={}):
    '''
    Generates Huffman codes for characters in the tree.
    :param node: Root node of the Huffman tree.
    :param prefix: Prefix to append for each character.
    :param codebook: Dictionary for storing character codes.
    :return: Codebook mapping characters to their Huffman codes.
    '''
    if node is not None:
        if node.char is not None:
            codebook[node.char] = prefix
        generate_codes(node.left, prefix + '0', codebook)
        generate_codes(node.right, prefix + '1', codebook)
    return codebook

def huffman_encoding(text):
    '''
    Encodes a text string using Huffman coding.
    :param text: The input string to encode.
    :return: Encoded string and the root of the Huffman tree.
    '''
    root = build_huffman_tree(text)
    huffman_codes = generate_codes(root)
    encoded_string = ''.join(huffman_codes[char] for char in text)
    return encoded_string, root

def huffman_decoding(encoded_string, root):
    '''
    Decodes a Huffman encoded string.
    :param encoded_string: The encoded string.
    :param root: The root of the Huffman tree for decoding.
    :return: Decoded string.
    '''
    decoded_string = []
    node = root
    for bit in encoded_string:
        node = node.left if bit == '0' else node.right
        if node.left is None and node.right is None:  # Leaf node
            decoded_string.append(node.char)
```

```
            node = root

    return ''.join(decoded_string)

# Example usage
if __name__ == "__main__":
    text = "this is an example for huffman encoding"
    encoded_string, tree_root = huffman_encoding(text)
    print(f"Encoded: {encoded_string}")
    decoded_string = huffman_decoding(encoded_string, tree_root)
    print(f"Decoded: {decoded_string}")
```

This code defines several key functions necessary for the implementation of Huffman coding:

- **HuffmanNode** class is used to represent each node in the Huffman tree.

- **build_huffman_tree** function constructs the Huffman tree using a priority queue (min-heap) which is essential for obtaining the optimal encoding.

- **generate_codes** function recursively generates the Huffman codes for each character and stores them in a codebook (dictionary).

- **huffman_encoding** function encodes a given text using the generated Huffman codes.

- **huffman_decoding** function decodes an encoded string back to its original form using the Huffman tree.

The final block of code provides an example of encoding and decoding a sample text string using the Huffman algorithm.

Chapter 30

Lempel-Ziv-Welch (LZW) Compression Algorithm

Below is a Python code snippet that showcases the implementation of the Lempel-Ziv-Welch (LZW) compression algorithm. This algorithm builds and uses a dictionary of substrings as part of its encoding process.

```python
def lzw_compress(uncompressed):
    """
    Compress a string to a list of output symbols using LZW.
    :param uncompressed: A string to be compressed.
    :return: A list of integers representing compressed input.
    """
    # Build the dictionary.
    dict_size = 256
    dictionary = {chr(i): i for i in range(dict_size)}

    w = ""
    result = []

    for c in uncompressed:
        wc = w + c
        if wc in dictionary:
            w = wc
        else:
            result.append(dictionary[w])
            # Add wc to the dictionary.
            dictionary[wc] = dict_size
            dict_size += 1
```

```
                w = c

        # Output the code for w.
        if w:
            result.append(dictionary[w])

        return result

def lzw_decompress(compressed):
    """
    Decompress a list of output ks to a string using LZW.
    :param compressed: A list of integers to be decompressed.
    :return: The decompressed string.
    """
    # Build the dictionary.
    dict_size = 256
    dictionary = {i: chr(i) for i in range(dict_size)}

    w = result = chr(compressed.pop(0))
    for k in compressed:
        if k in dictionary:
            entry = dictionary[k]
        elif k == dict_size:
            entry = w + w[0]
        else:
            raise ValueError(f"Bad compressed k: {k}")

        result += entry

        # Add w+entry[0] to the dictionary.
        dictionary[dict_size] = w + entry[0]
        dict_size += 1

        w = entry

    return result

# Example usage:
compressed_data = lzw_compress("TOBEORNOTTOBEORTOBEORNOT")
print("Compressed:", compressed_data)
decompressed_data = lzw_decompress(compressed_data)
print("Decompressed:", decompressed_data)
```

This code defines the essential functions to implement LZW compression and decompression:

- `lzw_compress` function compresses the input string into a list of integers, maintaining a dynamic dictionary of previously encountered substrings.

- `lzw_decompress` takes the list of compressed integers and

95

rebuilds the original string, using an expanding dictionary similar to the compression process.

In the example usage, the input string "TOBEORNOTTOBE-ORTOBEORNOT" is compressed and then decompressed, demonstrating the LZW algorithm's functionality in Python.

Chapter 31

Burrows-Wheeler Transform in Data Compression

Below is a Python code snippet that delves into the computation aspects of the Burrows-Wheeler Transform (BWT), demonstrating both the transformation and inversion processes.

```python
def bwt_transform(input_string):
    '''
    Perform the Burrows-Wheeler Transform on the input string.
    :param input_string: Original string to be transformed.
    :return: Transformed string (BWT).
    '''
    # Append the EOF character to ensure it's the last entry
    eof_char = "$"
    input_string += eof_char

    # Generate all rotations of the string
    rotations = [input_string[i:] + input_string[:i] for i in
    ↪    range(len(input_string))]

    # Sort the rotations
    rotations.sort()

    # Form the transformed string by taking the last char from each
    ↪    rotation
    transformed = ''.join(rotation[-1] for rotation in rotations)

    return transformed
```

```
def bwt_inverse(transformed_string):
    '''
    Reconstruct the original string from its Burrows-Wheeler
    ↪ Transform.
    :param transformed_string: BWT of the original string.
    :return: Original string before transformation.
    '''
    n = len(transformed_string)
    table = [""] * n

    # Iteratively build the table of sorted rotations
    for _ in range(n):
        # Add transformed string as column to the left of each entry
        table = sorted([transformed_string[i] + table[i] for i in
        ↪ range(n)])

    # Find the row that ends with the EOF character and return it
    ↪ without the EOF
    for row in table:
        if row.endswith("$"):
            return row[:-1]

# Example usage:
original_string = "banana"
bwt_result = bwt_transform(original_string)
recovered_string = bwt_inverse(bwt_result)

print("Original:", original_string)
print("Transformed (BWT):", bwt_result)
print("Recovered:", recovered_string)
```

This code snippet encompasses the essential functions necessary for executing the Burrows-Wheeler Transform and its inversion:

- `bwt_transform` generates the transformed string by performing rotations, sorting them, and collecting the last column.

- `bwt_inverse` reconstructs the original string using the property of BWT that allows for sorting reconstruction.

The demonstration concludes with an example transformation and recovery for the input "banana."

Chapter 32

Arithmetic Coding for High-Performance Compression

Below is a Python code snippet that encompasses the core computational elements of arithmetic coding, including symbol probability handling, interval subdivision, and encoding logic.

```python
class ArithmeticCoding:
    def __init__(self, symbols, probabilities):
        '''
        Initialize the ArithmeticCoding with symbols and their
        ↪   probabilities.
        :param symbols: List of symbols to be encoded.
        :param probabilities: Corresponding probabilities for the
        ↪   symbols.
        '''
        self.symbols = symbols
        self.probabilities = probabilities
        self.cumulative_prob =
        ↪   self._cumulative_probabilities(probabilities)

    def _cumulative_probabilities(self, probabilities):
        '''
        Calculate cumulative probabilities from individual
        ↪   probabilities.
        :param probabilities: List of symbol probabilities.
        :return: Cumulative probability array.
        '''
        cumulative = [0] * len(probabilities)
        cumulative[0] = probabilities[0]
```

```python
        for i in range(1, len(probabilities)):
            cumulative[i] = cumulative[i-1] + probabilities[i]
        return cumulative

    def encode(self, message):
        '''
        Encode a message using arithmetic coding.
        :param message: The string to encode.
        :return: Encoded value.
        '''
        low, high = 0.0, 1.0
        for symbol in message:
            index = self.symbols.index(symbol)
            range_width = high - low
            high = low + range_width * self.cumulative_prob[index]
            low = low + range_width * (self.cumulative_prob[index] -
            ↪  self.probabilities[index])
        return (high + low) / 2

    def decode(self, encoded_value, message_length):
        '''
        Decode an encoded message using arithmetic coding.
        :param encoded_value: The encoded numeric value.
        :param message_length: Length of the original message.
        :return: The decoded message.
        '''
        message = []
        for _ in range(message_length):
            for i, symbol in enumerate(self.symbols):
                if self.cumulative_prob[i] - self.probabilities[i]
                ↪  <= encoded_value < self.cumulative_prob[i]:
                    message.append(symbol)
                    range_width = self.cumulative_prob[i] -
                    ↪  (self.cumulative_prob[i] -
                    ↪  self.probabilities[i])
                    encoded_value = (encoded_value -
                    ↪  (self.cumulative_prob[i] -
                    ↪  self.probabilities[i])) / range_width
                    break
        return ''.join(message)

# Example usage
symbols = ['a', 'b', 'c']
probabilities = [0.5, 0.3, 0.2]

ac = ArithmeticCoding(symbols, probabilities)

message = "abac"
encoded_value = ac.encode(message)
decoded_message = ac.decode(encoded_value, len(message))

print("Encoded Value:", encoded_value)
```

100

```
print("Decoded Message:", decoded_message)
```

This code defines several key functions and operations necessary for implementing arithmetic coding, handling probabilities, and encoding/decoding a message:

- `ArithmeticCoding` class initializes with the symbols and their respective probabilities.

- `_cumulative_probabilities` calculates the cumulative distribution required for interval subdivision.

- `encode` method compresses a given message into a numerical value considering probability intervals.

- `decode` method reconstructs the original message from the encoded numerical value.

The class provides a systematic approach to model the encoding and decoding processes of arithmetic coding, ensuring compression rates approach the theoretical limit imposed by entropy.

Chapter 33

Earley Parser for Complex Grammars

Below is a Python code snippet that implements the Earley parsing algorithm, which is capable of parsing all context-free grammars. This code can be applied to tasks such as natural language processing and compiler construction.

```python
class EarleyParser:
    def __init__(self, grammar):
        """
        Initialize the parser with a given grammar.
        :param grammar: A dictionary where keys are non-terminals
        ↪    and values are lists of lists representing productions.
        """
        self.grammar = grammar
        self.chart = []

    def predict(self, state, index):
        """
        Prediction operation: For a state with a non-terminal right
        ↪    after the dot, add its productions to the chart.
        :param state: The current state (X -> •Y, j).
        :param index: The index in the input string.
        """
        next_symbol = state[1][state[2]]
        for prod in self.grammar.get(next_symbol, []):
            new_state = (next_symbol, prod, 0, index)
            if new_state not in self.chart[index]:
                self.chart[index].append(new_state)

    def scan(self, state, token, index):
        """
```

```python
    Scanning operation: If the next symbol right after the dot
    ↪   is a terminal and matches the current token,
    move to the next state.
    :param state: The current state (X -> •a, j).
    :param token: The current token from the input string.
    :param index: The current index in the input string.
    """
    next_symbol = state[1][state[2]]
    if next_symbol == token:
        new_state = (state[0], state[1], state[2] + 1, state[3])
        if new_state not in self.chart[index + 1]:
            self.chart[index + 1].append(new_state)

def complete(self, state, index):
    """
    Completion operation: If the dot is at the end of a
    ↪   production, move the dot in the original state that
    predicted this production.
    :param state: The current state (X -> •, j).
    :param index: The index in the input string.
    """
    for prev_state in self.chart[state[3]]:
        before_dot = prev_state[2]
        if before_dot < len(prev_state[1]) and
        ↪   prev_state[1][before_dot] == state[0]:
            new_state = (prev_state[0], prev_state[1],
            ↪   before_dot + 1, prev_state[3])
            if new_state not in self.chart[index]:
                self.chart[index].append(new_state)

def parse(self, tokens):
    """
    Parse a list of input tokens using the Earley algorithm.
    :param tokens: The input tokens to be parsed.
    :return: True if the tokens can be parsed according to the
    ↪   grammar, False otherwise.
    """
    self.chart = [[] for _ in range(len(tokens) + 1)]
    start_symbol = list(self.grammar.keys())[0]

    # Initial state to the chart
    start_state = (start_symbol, self.grammar[start_symbol][0],
    ↪   0, 0)
    self.chart[0].append(start_state)

    # Process each token
    for i, token in enumerate(tokens + [None]):   # Adding None
    ↪   to handle situation after last token
        for state in self.chart[i]:
            # if completed state
            if state[2] == len(state[1]):
                self.complete(state, i)
            # if the next symbol is non-terminal
```

103

```
                elif state[1][state[2]] in self.grammar:
                    self.predict(state, i)
                # if the next symbol is terminal
                elif i < len(tokens):
                    self.scan(state, tokens[i], i)

        # Check if the input is successfully parsed
        for state in self.chart[len(tokens)]:
            if state[0] == start_symbol and state[2] ==
            ↪  len(state[1]) and state[3] == 0:
                return True

        return False

# Example grammar (S -> NP VP, NP -> Det N, VP -> V NP)
example_grammar = {
    'S': [['NP', 'VP']],
    'NP': [['Det', 'N']],
    'VP': [['V', 'NP']],
    'Det': [['the']],
    'N': [['cat']],
    'V': [['saw']]
}

# Tokens from an input sentence "the cat saw the cat"
tokens = ['the', 'cat', 'saw', 'the', 'cat']

parser = EarleyParser(example_grammar)
result = parser.parse(tokens)
print("Parsed:", result)  # Output should be: Parsed: True if the
↪  sentence matches the grammar
```

This code defines an Earley parser for context-free grammars using a class structure:

- The **EarleyParser** class supports the operations: **predict**, **scan**, and **complete**, which form the core of the algorithm.

- The **parse** method applies these operations to parse an input sequence of tokens using the specified grammar.

- This implementation uses a simple grammar mapping sentences to parts of speech and can be modified for more complex grammars.

- Given a sequence of tokens from a sentence, the parser determines if it can be derived from the grammar.

The example demonstrates parsing a sentence with a basic grammar, returning **True** if the sentence complies with the defined structure.

Chapter 34

LALR Parser Generation for Programming Languages

Below is a Python code snippet that provides an implementation of an LALR(1) parser generator, which is used in compiler design for parsing context-free grammars with look-ahead capabilities. The code includes key functions for parsing table generation and conflict resolution.

```python
class Grammar:
    def __init__(self, start_symbol):
        self.start_symbol = start_symbol
        self.productions = {}
        self.non_terminals = set()
        self.terminals = set()

    def add_production(self, non_terminal, production):
        self.non_terminals.add(non_terminal)
        self.productions.setdefault(non_terminal,
        ↪ []).append(production)
        for symbol in production:
            if not symbol.isupper():
                self.terminals.add(symbol)

class LALRParser:
    def __init__(self, grammar):
```

```python
        self.grammar = grammar
        self.parse_table = {}
        self.states = []

    def compute_closure(self, items):
        closure = set(items)
        changed = True
        while changed:
            changed = False
            new_items = set(closure)
            for (lhs, rest, lookahead) in closure:
                if rest and rest[0] in self.grammar.non_terminals:
                    for prod in self.grammar.productions[rest[0]]:
                        new_item = (rest[0], prod, lookahead)
                        if new_item not in closure:
                            new_items.add(new_item)
                            changed = True
            closure = new_items
        return closure

    def compute_goto(self, state, symbol):
        goto_result = set()
        for (lhs, rest, lookahead) in state:
            if rest and rest[0] == symbol:
                goto_result.add((lhs, rest[1:], lookahead))
        return self.compute_closure(goto_result)

    def generate_states(self):
        start_item = (self.grammar.start_symbol,
        ↪   self.grammar.productions[self.grammar.start_symbol][0],
        ↪   '$')
        initial_state = self.compute_closure([start_item])
        self.states.append(initial_state)
        while True:
            new_states = self.states[:]
            for state in self.states:
                for symbol in
                ↪   self.grammar.non_terminals.union(self.grammar.terminals):
                    new_state = self.compute_goto(state, symbol)
                    if new_state and new_state not in new_states:
                        new_states.append(new_state)
            if new_states == self.states:
                break
            else:
                self.states = new_states

    def build_parse_table(self):
        self.generate_states()
        for index, state in enumerate(self.states):
            self.parse_table[index] = {}
            for item in state:
                lhs, rest, lookahead = item
                if not rest:
```

```
                    if lhs == self.grammar.start_symbol:
                        self.parse_table[index][lookahead] =
                        ↪   'accept'
                    else:
                        self.parse_table[index][lookahead] =
                        ↪   f'reduce {lhs} -> {" ".join(rest)}'
                else:
                    next_symbol = rest[0]
                    goto_state = self.compute_goto(state,
                    ↪   next_symbol)
                    if goto_state in self.states:
                        self.parse_table[index][next_symbol] =
                        ↪   self.states.index(goto_state)

    def parse_input(self, input_tokens):
        stack = [0]  # Initial state
        tokens = input_tokens + ['$']
        index = 0
        while index < len(tokens):
            state = stack[-1]
            current_token = tokens[index]
            action = self.parse_table[state].get(current_token)

            if action is None:
                raise SyntaxError('Parsing Error: Unexpected token')

            if action == 'accept':
                return 'Input accepted'
            elif action.startswith('shift'):
                stack.append(int(action.split()[1]))
                index += 1
            elif action.startswith('reduce'):
                _, prod_rule = action.split(' ', 1)
                lhs, rhs = prod_rule.split('->')
                rhs_symbols = rhs.split()
                for _ in rhs_symbols:
                    stack.pop()

                ↪   stack.append(self.parse_table[stack[-1]][lhs.strip()])
        raise SyntaxError('Parsing Error: Incomplete parsing')


# Example usage
grammar = Grammar("S")
grammar.add_production("S", ["E"])
grammar.add_production("E", ["E", "+", "T"])
grammar.add_production("E", ["T"])
grammar.add_production("T", ["id"])

lalr_parser = LALRParser(grammar)
lalr_parser.build_parse_table()
result = lalr_parser.parse_input(["id", "+", "id"])
```

```
print(result)  # Output: Input accepted
```

This code defines several key components for implementing an LALR(1) parser:

- **Grammar** class encapsulates a context-free grammar, including productions and terminal/non-terminal symbol classification.

- **LALRParser** class provides functionality to build and manipulate parsing tables for LALR parsing, including closure and goto calculations.

- **compute_closure** determines the closure of a set of LR(0) items, crucial for state building.

- **compute_goto** computes the GOTO function for state transitions in the parsing process.

- **build_parse_table** generates the parse table necessary for LALR(1) parsing by iterating over states and input symbols.

- **parse_input** performs the parsing of a given token sequence using the generated parse table and stack-based approach.

The final block of code demonstrates how this LALR(1) parser can be used with a simple grammar and input sequence to produce parsing results.

Chapter 35

LL Parsing Techniques for Recursive Descent Parsers

Below is a Python code snippet that demonstrates the construction of an LL(1) parser. The code includes building a parsing table, checking for left recursion and removing it, and parsing a given input string using the constructed parser.

```python
# LL(1) Parser Implementation

def remove_left_recursion(non_terminal, productions):
    """
    Eliminate left recursion from the grammar.

    :param non_terminal: The recursive non-terminal symbol.
    :param productions: Production rules for the non-terminal.
    :return: New non-left-recursive production rules.
    """
    alpha = []
    beta = []
    new_productions = {}

    for production in productions:
        # Distinguish between left-recursive (alpha) and
        ↪   non-left-recursive (beta) production
        if production.startswith(non_terminal):
            alpha.append(production[1:])
        else:
            beta.append(production)
```

```python
    if alpha:
        new_non_terminal = non_terminal + "'"
        new_productions[non_terminal] = [
            b + new_non_terminal for b in beta] + ([''] if not beta
            ↪ else [])
        new_productions[new_non_terminal] = [a + new_non_terminal
        ↪ for a in alpha] + ['']
    else:
        new_productions[non_terminal] = productions

    return new_productions

def construct_ll1_table(productions, first_sets, follow_sets):
    """
    Construct LL(1) parsing table.

    :param productions: Dict of production rules for each
    ↪ non-terminal.
    :param first_sets: First set for each non-terminal.
    :param follow_sets: Follow set for each non-terminal.
    :return: LL(1) parsing table.
    """
    table = {}

    for non_terminal, rules in productions.items():
        for rule in rules:
            first = first_sets[rule[0]]
            for terminal in first:
                table[(non_terminal, terminal)] = rule

            if '' in first:
                for terminal in follow_sets[non_terminal]:
                    table[(non_terminal, terminal)] = rule

    return table

def parse_input_string(ll1_table, start_symbol, input_string):
    """
    Parse the input string using the LL(1) parsing table.

    :param ll1_table: The parsing table.
    :param start_symbol: The start symbol of the grammar.
    :param input_string: The input string to parse.
    :return: Success or failure result of parsing.
    """
    stack = [start_symbol]
    index = 0
    input_tokens = input_string.split()

    while stack:
        top = stack.pop()

        if top == '':
```

110

```
            continue
        elif top in lll_table:
            rule = lll_table.get((top, input_tokens[index]))
            if rule:
                stack.extend(reversed(rule))
            else:
                return "Parsing Error: No rule found."
        elif top == input_tokens[index]:
            index += 1
        else:
            return f"Parsing Error: Expected {top}, found
            ↪   {input_tokens[index]}."

    if index == len(input_tokens):
        return "Parsing Successful."
    else:
        return "Parsing Error: Input not fully consumed."

# Example grammar and input, typically provided
productions = {
    'E': ['TX'],
    'X': ['+TX', ''],
    'T': ['FY'],
    'Y': ['*FY', ''],
    'F': ['(E)', 'a']
}

first_sets = {
    'E': {'(', 'a'},
    'X': {'+', ''},
    'T': {'(', 'a'},
    'Y': {'*', ''},
    'F': {'(', 'a'},
    '(': {'('},
    'a': {'a'},
    '+': {'+'},
    '*': {'*'},
    '': {''}
}

follow_sets = {
    'E': {')', '$'},
    'X': {')', '$'},
    'T': {'+', ')', '$'},
    'Y': {'+', ')', '$'},
    'F': {'*', '+', ')', '$'}
}

start_symbol = 'E'
input_string = "( a + a ) * a $"
lll_table = construct_lll_table(productions, first_sets,
↪   follow_sets)
```

```
output = parse_input_string(lll_table, start_symbol, input_string)
print(output)
```

This code outlines the essential steps for implementing an LL(1) parser:

- **remove_left_recursion** function eliminates left recursion from a given set of production rules, which is necessary to obtain an LL(1) grammar.

- **construct_lll_table** uses the provided production, first, and follow sets to construct a parsing table.

- **parse_input_string** takes the LL(1) parsing table and attempts to parse a given input string, returning success or detailed error messages.

The example grammar and input are used to demonstrate parsing and show how an input string can be successfully analyzed in accordance with the grammatical rules defined.

Chapter 36

RSA Algorithm for Public-Key Cryptography

Below is a Python code snippet that demonstrates key aspects of the RSA algorithm, including key generation, encryption, and decryption processes.

```python
import random

def gcd(a, b):
    '''Compute the greatest common divisor of a and b.'''
    while b:
        a, b = b, a % b
    return a

def multiplicative_inverse(e, phi):
    '''Compute the multiplicative inverse of e modulo phi.'''
    x0, x1, y0, y1 = 0, 1, 1, 0
    original_phi = phi
    while phi != 0:
        q, e, phi = e // phi, phi, e % phi
        x0, x1 = x1 - q * x0, x0
        y0, y1 = y1 - q * y0, y0
    if e != 1:
        raise ValueError("No modular inverse exists.")
    return x1 % original_phi

def is_prime(num):
    '''Determine if num is a prime number.'''
    if num < 2:
```

```
        return False
    for n in range(2, int(num ** 0.5) + 1):
        if num % n == 0:
            return False
    return True

def generate_keypair(p, q):
    '''Generate a pair of RSA keys.'''
    if not (is_prime(p) and is_prime(q)):
        raise ValueError("Both numbers must be prime.")
    elif p == q:
        raise ValueError("p and q must be different.")

    n = p * q
    phi = (p - 1) * (q - 1)

    e = random.randrange(2, phi)
    g = gcd(e, phi)
    while g != 1:
        e = random.randrange(2, phi)
        g = gcd(e, phi)

    d = multiplicative_inverse(e, phi)

    return ((e, n), (d, n))

def encrypt(pk, plaintext):
    '''Encrypt plaintext using a public key.'''
    key, n = pk
    cipher = [(ord(char) ** key) % n for char in plaintext]
    return cipher

def decrypt(pk, ciphertext):
    '''Decrypt ciphertext using a private key.'''
    key, n = pk
    plain = [chr((char ** key) % n) for char in ciphertext]
    return ''.join(plain)

# Example usage of RSA
p = 61  # Example prime number
q = 53  # Example prime number
public, private = generate_keypair(p, q)
message = "HELLO"
encrypted_msg = encrypt(public, message)
decrypted_msg = decrypt(private, encrypted_msg)

print("Message:", message)
print("Encrypted:", encrypted_msg)
print("Decrypted:", decrypted_msg)
```

This code provides foundational functionality for RSA encryption and decryption:

- **gcd** function computes the greatest common divisor of two integers, essential for ensuring that the chosen e is coprime with $\phi(n)$.

- **multiplicative_inverse** calculates the modular inverse, crucial for determining the decryption exponent d.

- **is_prime** checks for primality, ensuring the prime status of inputs p and q.

- **generate_keypair** produces a pair of RSA keys (public and private) based on prime inputs.

- **encrypt** and **decrypt** functions manage the encryption and decryption processes using RSA's mathematical principles.

The example demonstrates how the functions can be utilized to encrypt and decrypt messages securely.

Chapter 37

Diffie-Hellman Key Exchange Protocol

Below is a Python code snippet that demonstrates the core computational principles of the Diffie-Hellman key exchange algorithm using modular arithmetic and discrete logarithms for secure key exchange over an insecure channel.

```python
import random

def generate_private_key(prime_modulus):
    '''
    Generate a private key.
    :param prime_modulus: Prime modulus for key generation.
    :return: Random private key.
    '''
    return random.randint(2, prime_modulus - 2)

def generate_public_key(base, private_key, prime_modulus):
    '''
    Generate a public key using the private key.
    :param base: Base (generator) for public key computation.
    :param private_key: Private key for exponential computation.
    :param prime_modulus: Prime modulus for calculation.
    :return: Public key.
    '''
    return pow(base, private_key, prime_modulus)

def compute_shared_key(public_key, private_key, prime_modulus):
    '''
    Compute shared key using received public key and own private
    ↪ key.
    :param public_key: Received public key.
```

```
    :param private_key: Own private key.
    :param prime_modulus: Prime modulus for calculation.
    :return: Shared secret key.
    '''
    return pow(public_key, private_key, prime_modulus)

def diffie_hellman_key_exchange(prime_modulus, base):
    '''
    Perform Diffie-Hellman key exchange.
    :param prime_modulus: Agreed prime modulus.
    :param base: Agreed base (generator).
    :return: Shared secret key.
    '''
    # Alice creates her private and public keys
    private_key_alice = generate_private_key(prime_modulus)
    public_key_alice = generate_public_key(base, private_key_alice,
    ↪   prime_modulus)

    # Bob creates his private and public keys
    private_key_bob = generate_private_key(prime_modulus)
    public_key_bob = generate_public_key(base, private_key_bob,
    ↪   prime_modulus)

    # Exchange of public keys would happen here

    # Each computes the shared secret
    shared_key_alice = compute_shared_key(public_key_bob,
    ↪   private_key_alice, prime_modulus)
    shared_key_bob = compute_shared_key(public_key_alice,
    ↪   private_key_bob, prime_modulus)

    assert shared_key_alice == shared_key_bob, "Shared keys do not
    ↪   match!"
    return shared_key_alice

# Define prime modulus and base typically agreed beforehand
prime_modulus = 23  # Example prime modulus
base = 5  # Example base (generator)

# Perform key exchange
shared_secret = diffie_hellman_key_exchange(prime_modulus, base)
print("Shared Secret Key:", shared_secret)
```

This code outlines the core functions and processes involved in
executing the Diffie-Hellman key exchange:

- generate_private_key function generates a private key randomly within the constraints of the prime modulus.

- generate_public_key calculates a public key using the base
  and private key, applying modular exponentiation.

- `compute_shared_key` derives the shared secret key using another's public key and the user's private key.

- `diffie_hellman_key_exchange` orchestrates the overall key exchange process, verifying that both parties derive the same shared secret.

This script simulates the steps both parties take to securely negotiate a shared key over an insecure channel, ensuring confidentiality without exchanging the private keys.

Chapter 38

Elliptic Curve Cryptography Algorithms

Below is a Python code snippet that implements the Elliptic Curve Cryptography (ECC) algorithms, including key generation and encryption using the popular library **cryptography**. The example demonstrates fundamental operations involved in ECC like key creation, signing, and verification.

```python
from cryptography.hazmat.primitives.asymmetric import ec
from cryptography.hazmat.primitives import hashes, serialization
from cryptography.exceptions import InvalidSignature

def generate_keys():
    '''
    Generate an ECC private and public key pair.
    :return: Tuple containing the private and public key.
    '''
    private_key = ec.generate_private_key(ec.SECP256R1()) # Using
    ↪    the SECP256R1 curve
    public_key = private_key.public_key()
    return private_key, public_key

def sign_data(private_key, data):
    '''
    Sign data using EC private key.
    :param private_key: The EC private key for signing.
    :param data: Data to be signed (as bytes).
    :return: Signature (as bytes).
```

```
    '''
    signature = private_key.sign(data, ec.ECDSA(hashes.SHA256()))
    return signature

def verify_signature(public_key, signature, data):
    '''
    Verify an EC signature.
    :param public_key: The EC public key for verification.
    :param signature: Signature to verify (as bytes).
    :param data: Original data (as bytes).
    :return: Boolean indicating the validity of the signature.
    '''
    try:
        public_key.verify(signature, data,
        ↪  ec.ECDSA(hashes.SHA256()))
        return True
    except InvalidSignature:
        return False

def serialize_key(key, private=False):
    '''
    Serialize an EC key to PEM format.
    :param key: The key to serialize (either private or public).
    :private: Boolean indicating if the key is private.
    :return: Serialized key in PEM format (as bytes).
    '''
    if private:
        return key.private_bytes(
            encoding=serialization.Encoding.PEM,
            format=serialization.PrivateFormat.TraditionalOpenSSL,
            encryption_algorithm=serialization.NoEncryption()
        )
    else:
        return key.public_bytes(
            encoding=serialization.Encoding.PEM,
            format=serialization.PublicFormat.SubjectPublicKeyInfo
        )

# Example usage
data = b'Hello, ECC!'
private_key, public_key = generate_keys()
signature = sign_data(private_key, data)
is_valid = verify_signature(public_key, signature, data)

private_key_pem = serialize_key(private_key, private=True)
public_key_pem = serialize_key(public_key)

print("Private Key:\n", private_key_pem.decode())
print("Public Key:\n", public_key_pem.decode())
print("Signature is valid:", is_valid)
```

This code defines several key functions necessary for operations using elliptic curve cryptography:

- **generate_keys** creates an EC private and public key pair suitable for signing and encryption operations.

- **sign_data** utilizes a private key to generate a digital signature of the provided data using the **ECDSA** signature algorithm.

- **verify_signature** checks the validity of a given signature using the associated public key to ensure data integrity and authenticity.

- **serialize_key** converts the keys into a PEM format for storage or transmission, supporting both private and public keys.

The final block provides an example of generating keys, signing data, verifying a signature, and serializing the keys into PEM format for demonstration purposes.

Chapter 39

Advanced Encryption Standard (AES) Algorithm

Below is a Python code snippet that provides an implementation of the Advanced Encryption Standard (AES) algorithm. The code encompasses all core aspects of the AES including key expansion, encryption, and decryption operations.

```python
from Crypto.Cipher import AES
from Crypto.Util.Padding import pad, unpad
import os

def generate_key_and_iv(key_size):
    '''
    Generate a random AES key and initialization vector (IV).
    :param key_size: Size of the AES key in bytes (16, 24, or 32).
    :return: Tuple of key and IV.
    '''
    key = os.urandom(key_size)
    iv = os.urandom(16)   # AES block size is 16 bytes
    return key, iv

def aes_encrypt(plaintext, key, iv):
    '''
    Encrypt a plaintext using AES encryption.
    :param plaintext: The data to encrypt (can be of any length).
    :param key: The AES key used for encryption.
    :param iv: The initialization vector.
    :return: Encrypted data.
    '''
```

```
    cipher = AES.new(key, AES.MODE_CBC, iv)
    ciphertext = cipher.encrypt(pad(plaintext, AES.block_size))
    return ciphertext

def aes_decrypt(ciphertext, key, iv):
    '''
    Decrypt an AES encrypted ciphertext.
    :param ciphertext: The encrypted data.
    :param key: The AES key used for decryption.
    :param iv: The initialization vector.
    :return: Decrypted plaintext.
    '''
    cipher = AES.new(key, AES.MODE_CBC, iv)
    plaintext = unpad(cipher.decrypt(ciphertext), AES.block_size)
    return plaintext

# Demonstration of AES encryption and decryption
def demo_aes():
    key_size = 32   # AES-256
    key, iv = generate_key_and_iv(key_size)
    print("Generated Key:", key.hex())
    print("Generated IV:", iv.hex())

    original_text = b"Secret Message"
    print("Original Text:", original_text)

    encrypted_text = aes_encrypt(original_text, key, iv)
    print("Encrypted Text:", encrypted_text.hex())

    decrypted_text = aes_decrypt(encrypted_text, key, iv)
    print("Decrypted Text:", decrypted_text)

# Run the demonstration
demo_aes()
```

This code defines several key operations needed for the AES encryption and decryption process:

- **generate_key_and_iv** generates a random AES key and initialization vector (IV) for the encryption.

- **aes_encrypt** performs AES encryption on the given plaintext using a provided key and IV. It applies padding to ensure the plaintext is a multiple of the block size.

- **aes_decrypt** decrypts the ciphertext back into plaintext by reversing the encryption process and removing the padding.

- **demo_aes** is a demonstration function that showcases the generation of a key and IV, encryption of a plaintext message, and decryption back to the original message.

These functions encapsulate the AES operations and demonstrate their application in Python for secure data encryption and decryption.

Chapter 40

Backpropagation Algorithm in Neural Networks

Below is a Python code snippet that encompasses the core computational elements of the backpropagation algorithm for training artificial neural networks, including forward pass, loss computation, backpropagation, and weight updates using gradient descent.

```python
import numpy as np

# Sigmoid activation function
def sigmoid(x):
    return 1 / (1 + np.exp(-x))

# Derivative of the sigmoid function
def sigmoid_derivative(x):
    return sigmoid(x) * (1 - sigmoid(x))

# Mean squared error loss function
def mean_squared_error(y_true, y_pred):
    return np.mean((y_true - y_pred) ** 2)

# Layer class representing each layer in the neural network
class Layer:
    def __init__(self, input_size, output_size):
        self.weights = np.random.rand(input_size, output_size) * 0.1
        self.biases = np.zeros((1, output_size))
        self.input = None
        self.output = None
```

```python
    def forward(self, input_data):
        self.input = input_data
        self.output = sigmoid(np.dot(self.input, self.weights) +
        ↪    self.biases)
        return self.output

    def backward(self, output_error, learning_rate):
        input_error = np.dot(output_error, self.weights.T)
        weights_error = np.dot(self.input.T, output_error)

        # Update weights and biases using gradient descent
        self.weights -= learning_rate * weights_error
        self.biases -= learning_rate * output_error
        return input_error

# NeuralNetwork class implementing the backpropagation algorithm
class NeuralNetwork:
    def __init__(self, learning_rate=0.01):
        self.layers = []
        self.learning_rate = learning_rate

    def add_layer(self, layer):
        self.layers.append(layer)

    def predict(self, input_data):
        output = input_data
        for layer in self.layers:
            output = layer.forward(output)
        return output

    def train(self, x_train, y_train, epochs):
        for epoch in range(epochs):
            for x, y in zip(x_train, y_train):
                # Forward pass
                output = self.predict(x)

                # Compute the loss (Error)
                error = output - y

                # Backward pass
                for layer in reversed(self.layers):
                    error = layer.backward(error *
                    ↪    sigmoid_derivative(layer.output),
                                           self.learning_rate)

            # Calculate mean squared error for the epoch
            mse = mean_squared_error(y_train, self.predict(x_train))
            print(f'Epoch {epoch+1}/{epochs}, MSE: {mse}')

# Example usage
if __name__ == "__main__":
    # Input dataset
    x_train = np.array([[0, 0],
```

```
                    [0, 1],
                    [1, 0],
                    [1, 1]])
# Labels (for XOR)
y_train = np.array([[0],
                    [1],
                    [1],
                    [0]])

# Create neural network
nn = NeuralNetwork(learning_rate=0.1)
nn.add_layer(Layer(2, 3))   # Add an input layer with 2 inputs
↪   and 3 neurons
nn.add_layer(Layer(3, 1))   # Add an output layer with 1 neuron

# Train the neural network
nn.train(x_train, y_train, epochs=1000)
```

This code defines several key components necessary for a functional neural network using the backpropagation algorithm:

- **Layer** class represents a single layer of the neural network and includes methods for forward and backward passes.

- **NeuralNetwork** class allows the creation and training of a multi-layer neural network, managing the sequence of operations from input to output.

- **sigmoid** and **sigmoid_derivative** functions are used as the activation function and its derivative, respectively.

- **mean_squared_error** function calculates the error between the predicted and true values.

In the **train** function, the network is iteratively optimized for a given number of epochs over the training data, gradually learning the relationship between inputs and outputs through weight and bias adjustments.

Chapter 41

Support Vector Machines for Classification

Below is a Python code snippet demonstrating the use of Support Vector Machine (SVM) algorithms with kernel tricks for handling non-linearly separable data. The implementation includes training an SVM model with the radial basis function (RBF) kernel and predicting on test data.

```python
from sklearn import datasets
from sklearn.model_selection import train_test_split
from sklearn.preprocessing import StandardScaler
from sklearn.svm import SVC
from sklearn.metrics import accuracy_score, classification_report

# Load example dataset
iris = datasets.load_iris()
X, y = iris.data, iris.target

# Standardize the dataset
scaler = StandardScaler()
X_scaled = scaler.fit_transform(X)

# Split the dataset into training and testing sets
X_train, X_test, y_train, y_test = train_test_split(X_scaled, y,
 ↪  test_size=0.3, random_state=42)

# Instantiate the SVM classifier with RBF kernel
svm_classifier = SVC(kernel='rbf', gamma='scale', C=1.0)
```

```
# Train the SVM classifier
svm_classifier.fit(X_train, y_train)

# Make predictions on the test data
y_pred = svm_classifier.predict(X_test)

# Evaluate the model performance
accuracy = accuracy_score(y_test, y_pred)
report = classification_report(y_test, y_pred)

print("Accuracy of the SVM classifier:", accuracy)
print("Classification Report:\n", report)
```

This code provides a practical example of employing a Support Vector Machine classifier for a classification task with the following core components:

- **StandardScaler** is used to standardize the dataset, ensuring features have a mean of zero and a standard deviation of one.

- **train_test_split** divides the dataset into training and testing subsets to evaluate model generalization.

- **SVC** from **sklearn** is instantiated with an RBF kernel, a popular choice for non-linear boundaries in data.

- **fit** and **predict** methods train the SVM model and obtain predictions on unseen data.

- **accuracy_score** and **classification_report** provide metrics to assess classifier performance, including overall accuracy, precision, recall, and F1-score.

This snippet highlights the use of kernel tricks in SVMs, which allows for effective handling of complex decision boundaries in feature space by transforming data into higher dimensions.

Chapter 42

K-Means Clustering Algorithm

Below is a Python code snippet that demonstrates the core computational elements of the K-means clustering algorithm including the initialization of centroids, iteration for convergence, and optimization criteria.

```python
import numpy as np
from sklearn.metrics import pairwise_distances_argmin
import matplotlib.pyplot as plt

def kmeans(X, n_clusters, n_init=10, max_iter=300):
    '''
    K-means clustering algorithm.
    :param X: The data to cluster.
    :param n_clusters: Number of clusters.
    :param n_init: Number of time the k-means algorithm will be run
    ↪    with different centroid seeds.
    :param max_iter: Maximum number of iterations of the k-means
    ↪    algorithm.
    :return: Tuple of (centroids, labels).
    '''
    best_inertia = None
    best_centroids = None
    best_labels = None

    for _ in range(n_init):
        # Randomly initialize the centroids as K random samples from
        ↪    the dataset
        centroids = X[np.random.choice(X.shape[0], n_clusters,
        ↪    replace=False)]
```

```
    for _ in range(max_iter):
        # Assign labels based on closest centroid
        labels = pairwise_distances_argmin(X, centroids)

        # Calculate new centroids as the mean of the points in
        ↪    each cluster
        new_centroids = np.array([X[labels == i].mean(axis=0)
        ↪    for i in range(n_clusters)])

        # Check for convergence
        if np.all(centroids == new_centroids):
            break

        centroids = new_centroids

    # Calculate inertia (sum of squared distances to closest
    ↪    centroid)
    inertia = np.sum((X - centroids[labels]) ** 2)

    if best_inertia is None or inertia < best_inertia:
        best_centroids = centroids
        best_labels = labels
        best_inertia = inertia

    return best_centroids, best_labels

def plot_kmeans(X, labels, centroids):
    '''
    Plots the data and the centroids computed by K-means.
    :param X: The data to plot.
    :param labels: Cluster labels for each point.
    :param centroids: Centroids of the clusters.
    '''
    plt.scatter(X[:, 0], X[:, 1], c=labels, s=50, cmap='viridis')
    plt.scatter(centroids[:, 0], centroids[:, 1], c='red', s=200,
    ↪    alpha=0.5)
    plt.show()

# Example usage
np.random.seed(0)
# Create sample data
X = np.random.rand(300, 2)

# Perform K-means clustering
centroids, labels = kmeans(X, n_clusters=3)

# Plot the resulting clusters
plot_kmeans(X, labels, centroids)
```

This code provides a complete implementation of the K-means clustering algorithm:

- The `kmeans` function initializes centroids, iteratively assigns points to clusters, recalculates centroids, and checks for convergence or inertia improvement.

- `plot_kmeans` helps visualize clustering results, depicting data points and centroids.

- The example provided demonstrates usage on randomly generated data, showcasing initialization, execution, and visualization of the algorithm's outcomes.

Chapter 43

Apriori Algorithm for Association Rule Learning

Below is a Python code snippet implementing the core mechanisms of the Apriori algorithm in data mining, focusing on the discovery of frequent itemsets and the generation of association rules. This implementation includes strategies for pruning candidate sets and improving performance.

```python
from itertools import combinations

def apriori(transactions, support_threshold):
    """
    Implementation of the Apriori algorithm to find frequent
    ↪    itemsets.
    :param transactions: List of transactions, where each
    ↪    transaction is a set of items.
    :param support_threshold: Minimum support threshold to consider
    ↪    an itemset as frequent.
    :return: List of frequent itemsets.
    """
    itemsets = {frozenset([item]) for transaction in transactions
    ↪    for item in transaction}
    current_itemsets = {itemset for itemset in itemsets if
                        sum(1 for transaction in transactions if
    ↪    itemset <= transaction) >=
    ↪    support_threshold}
    frequent_itemsets = []
```

```
    k = 2
    while current_itemsets:
        frequent_itemsets.extend(current_itemsets)
        current_itemsets = {frozenset(i.union(j)) for i in
        ↪   current_itemsets for j in current_itemsets
                            if len(i.union(j)) == k}
        current_itemsets = {itemset for itemset in current_itemsets
        ↪   if
                            sum(1 for transaction in transactions if
                            ↪   itemset <= transaction) >=
                            ↪   support_threshold}
        k += 1

    return frequent_itemsets

def generate_association_rules(frequent_itemsets, transactions,
↪   confidence_threshold):
    """
    Generate association rules from frequent itemsets.
    :param frequent_itemsets: List of frequent itemsets.
    :param transactions: List of transactions.
    :param confidence_threshold: Minimum confidence threshold to
    ↪   consider a rule.
    :return: List of association rules in the form of (antecedent,
    ↪   consequent, confidence).
    """
    rules = []
    transaction_list = list(map(set, transactions))

    for itemset in frequent_itemsets:
        for i in range(1, len(itemset)):
            for antecedent in combinations(itemset, i):
                antecedent = set(antecedent)
                consequent = itemset - antecedent
                support_antecedent = sum(1 for transaction in
                ↪   transaction_list if antecedent <= transaction)
                support_itemset = sum(1 for transaction in
                ↪   transaction_list if itemset <= transaction)

                confidence = support_itemset / support_antecedent
                if confidence >= confidence_threshold:
                    rules.append((antecedent, consequent,
                    ↪   confidence))

    return rules

# Example transaction data
transactions = [
    {'beer', 'nuts', 'chips'},
    {'beer', 'chips'},
    {'beer', 'nuts'},
    {'nuts', 'chips'},
    {'chips'}
```

```
]

# Define support and confidence thresholds
support_threshold = 2
confidence_threshold = 0.6

# Run Apriori algorithm
frequent_itemsets = apriori(transactions, support_threshold)
print("Frequent Itemsets:", frequent_itemsets)

# Generate association rules
rules = generate_association_rules(frequent_itemsets, transactions,
↪   confidence_threshold)
print("Association Rules:")
for antecedent, consequent, confidence in rules:
    print(f"Rule: {antecedent} -> {consequent}, confidence:
    ↪   {confidence:.2f}")
```

This code defines the following core functions essential for implementing the Apriori algorithm:

- `apriori` function discovers frequent itemsets by iteratively generating candidate sets and pruning infrequent ones based on a support threshold.

- `generate_association_rules` constructs association rules from frequent itemsets that have confidence above a predefined threshold.

Using the provided example transaction data, this code demonstrates the process of extracting frequent patterns and rules from transactional datasets, leveraging pruning strategies to improve computational efficiency.

Chapter 44

PageRank Algorithm for Web Search Ranking

Below is a Python code snippet that implements the core elements of the PageRank algorithm using the Markov chain model and power iteration method for iterative computation.

```python
import numpy as np

def create_transition_matrix(links, num_pages, damping_factor=0.85):
    """
    Create a transition probability matrix for a web link structure.
    :param links: List of tuples representing directed edges between
    ↪   pages (from, to).
    :param num_pages: Total number of web pages.
    :param damping_factor: Probability at which a user continues
    ↪   following links (usually 0.85).
    :return: Transition matrix.
    """
    # Initialize matrices
    transition_matrix = np.zeros((num_pages, num_pages),
    ↪   dtype=float)
    outlink_counts = np.zeros(num_pages, dtype=float)

    # Count outlinks for each page
    for (source, target) in links:
        transition_matrix[target, source] += 1.0
        outlink_counts[source] += 1.0

    # Construct probability distribution for each column
```

```python
        for j in range(num_pages):
            if outlink_counts[j] > 0:
                for i in range(num_pages):
                    transition_matrix[i, j] = (
                        (transition_matrix[i, j] / outlink_counts[j]) *
                        ↪  damping_factor
                        + (1.0 - damping_factor) / num_pages
                    )
            else:
                # Handle pages with no outlinks (sink nodes)
                transition_matrix[:, j] = 1.0 / num_pages

    return transition_matrix

def power_iteration(matrix, num_pages, epsilon=1e-6,
↪  max_iterations=100):
    """
    Compute PageRank vector using power iteration.
    :param matrix: Transition matrix.
    :param num_pages: Total number of web pages.
    :param epsilon: Convergence threshold.
    :param max_iterations: Maximum number of iterations.
    :return: PageRank vector.
    """
    # Initialize PageRank vector with equal probability
    pagerank = np.ones(num_pages) / num_pages
    for iteration in range(max_iterations):
        new_pagerank = np.dot(matrix, pagerank)
        # Check convergence
        if np.linalg.norm(new_pagerank - pagerank, 1) < epsilon:
            print(f"Converged after {iteration + 1} iterations.")
            break
        pagerank = new_pagerank

    return pagerank

# Example usage:
num_pages = 4
links = [(0, 1), (1, 2), (2, 3), (3, 0), (0, 2), (1, 3), (3, 1)]

transition_matrix = create_transition_matrix(links, num_pages)
pagerank_vector = power_iteration(transition_matrix, num_pages)

print("PageRank Values:", pagerank_vector)
```

This code defines functions for implementing the PageRank algorithm based on a Markov chain model:

- The `create_transition_matrix` function constructs a transition matrix that models the probability of transitioning from one web page to another in the network, incorporating damping to handle missing links.

- The `power_iteration` function applies power iteration to compute the steady-state PageRank vector, which indicates the relative importance of each page.

The example demonstrates setting up the transition matrix and calculating the PageRank values for a simple network of pages.

Chapter 45

Fibonacci Heap Data Structure

Below is a Python code snippet that demonstrates the core operations of a Fibonacci Heap, including insertion, union operations, and extraction of the minimum element. This example highlights key operations essential for network optimization algorithms.

```python
import math

class Node:
    def __init__(self, key):
        self.key = key
        self.degree = 0
        self.parent = None
        self.child = None
        self.mark = False
        self.next = self
        self.prev = self

class FibonacciHeap:
    def __init__(self):
        self.min = None
        self.count = 0

    def insert(self, key):
        node = Node(key)
        if self.min is None:
            self.min = node
        else:
            node.next = self.min
            node.prev = self.min.prev
            self.min.prev.next = node
```

```python
            self.min.prev = node
            if key < self.min.key:
                self.min = node
        self.count += 1
        return node

    def merge(self, other):
        if other.min is None:
            return self
        if self.min is None:
            self.min = other.min
        else:
            self.min.prev.next = other.min.next
            other.min.next.prev = self.min.prev
            self.min.prev = other.min
            other.min.next = self.min
            if other.min.key < self.min.key:
                self.min = other.min
        self.count += other.count
        return self

    def extract_min(self):
        z = self.min
        if z is not None:
            if z.child is not None:
                children = [x for x in self.iterate(z.child)]
                for child in children:
                    child.prev.next = child.next
                    child.next.prev = child.prev
                    child.next = self.min
                    child.prev = self.min.prev
                    self.min.prev.next = child
                    self.min.prev = child
                    child.parent = None
            z.prev.next = z.next
            z.next.prev = z.prev
            if z == z.next:
                self.min = None
            else:
                self.min = z.next
                self.consolidate()
            self.count -= 1
        return z

    def consolidate(self):
        max_degree = int(math.log(self.count) * math.log(2)) + 1
        A = [None] * max_degree

        nodes = [x for x in self.iterate(self.min)]
        for w in nodes:
            x = w
            d = x.degree
            while A[d] is not None:
```

140

```
                y = A[d]
                if x.key > y.key:
                    x, y = y, x
                self.link(y, x)
                A[d] = None
                d += 1
            A[d] = x

        self.min = None
        for i in range(max_degree):
            if A[i] is not None:
                if self.min is None:
                    self.min = A[i]
                else:
                    A[i].prev.next = A[i].next
                    A[i].next.prev = A[i].prev
                    A[i].next = self.min
                    A[i].prev = self.min.prev
                    self.min.prev.next = A[i]
                    self.min.prev = A[i]
                    if A[i].key < self.min.key:
                        self.min = A[i]

    @staticmethod
    def link(y, x):
        y.prev.next = y.next
        y.next.prev = y.prev
        y.next = y.prev = y
        if x.child is None:
            x.child = y
        else:
            y.next = x.child
            y.prev = x.child.prev
            x.child.prev.next = y
            x.child.prev = y
        y.parent = x
        x.degree += 1
        y.mark = False

    def iterate(self, head):
        node = stop = head
        flag = False
        while True:
            if node is head and flag:
                break
            elif node is head:
                flag = True

            yield node
            node = node.next

# Example usage
fib_heap = FibonacciHeap()
```

```
fib_heap.insert(3)
fib_heap.insert(7)
fib_heap.insert(24)
min_node = fib_heap.extract_min()
print("Minimum:", min_node.key if min_node else "Heap is empty")  #
↪    Outputs the minimum key
```

This code defines a Fibonacci Heap with essential operations to support network optimization algorithms:

- `insert` function adds a new element to the heap.

- `merge` combines two Fibonacci heaps into one.

- `extract_min` removes and returns the node with the smallest key.

- `consolidate` restructures the heap after extraction to maintain the heap property.

- `link` is used to combine trees of the same degree.

- `iterate` aids in iterating through circular doubly-linked lists.

The example at the end demonstrates the insertion of elements into the Fibonacci Heap and the extraction of the minimum element.

Chapter 46

Bloom Filters for Probabilistic Data Representation

Below is a Python code snippet that demonstrates the implementation and usage of a Bloom filter, which is a space-efficient probabilistic data structure used for set membership queries.

```python
import math
import hashlib

class BloomFilter:
    def __init__(self, size, hash_count):
        '''
        Initialize the Bloom Filter.
        :param size: The size of the bloom filter.
        :param hash_count: The number of hash functions to use.
        '''
        self.size = size
        self.hash_count = hash_count
        self.bit_array = [0] * size

    def _hashes(self, item):
        '''
        Generates hash values using multiple hash functions.
        :param item: The item to hash.
        :return: A generator yielding hash values.
        '''
        for i in range(self.hash_count):
            # We create a unique hash for each function by using a
            ↪   seed (i)
```

```python
        yield
        ↪   int(hashlib.sha256(item.encode('utf-8')).hexdigest(),
        ↪   16) % self.size

    def add(self, item):
        '''
        Add an item to the bloom filter.
        :param item: The item to add.
        '''
        for hash_value in self._hashes(item):
            self.bit_array[hash_value] = 1

    def __contains__(self, item):
        '''
        Check if an item is in the bloom filter.
        :param item: The item to check.
        :return: Boolean indicating if item is potentially in the
        ↪   set.
        '''
        return all(self.bit_array[hash_value] for hash_value in
        ↪   self._hashes(item))

def optimal_size_and_hash(items_count, fp_prob):
    '''
    Calculates optimal bloom filter size and hash count.
    :param items_count: Number of items expected to be stored.
    :param fp_prob: Probability of false positives.
    :return: Tuple of size and number of hash functions.
    '''
    size = -int(items_count * math.log(fp_prob) / (math.log(2) **
    ↪   2))
    hash_count = int(size / items_count * math.log(2))
    return size, hash_count


# Example usage
n_items = 20
false_positive_probability = 0.05

# Get the optimal size and hash count
size, hash_count = optimal_size_and_hash(n_items,
↪   false_positive_probability)
bloom_filter = BloomFilter(size, hash_count)

# Adding items to the bloom filter
items_to_add = ["apple", "banana", "grape", "orange", "mango"]
for item in items_to_add:
    bloom_filter.add(item)

# Test membership
test_items = ["apple", "mango", "lemon", "orange"]
for item in test_items:
    if item in bloom_filter:
        print(f"{item} is probably in the bloom filter.")
```

```
else:
    print(f"{item} is definitely not in the bloom filter.")
```

This code defines the core functionality of a Bloom filter data structure:

- The `BloomFilter` class initializes the filter with a set size and the number of hash functions. It uses the `hashlib` library to generate multiple hash values for each item.

- The `_hashes` method generates multiple hash values for a given item, accommodating the customizable number of hash functions.

- The `add` method inserts items into the bloom filter by setting bits in an internal array based on generated hash values.

- The `__contains__` method checks for potential membership of an item by testing all relevant positions in the bit array.

- The standalone function `optimal_size_and_hash` computes the filter's optimal size and the number of hash functions required to achieve a specified false positive probability for a given number of expected items.

This design allows for efficient checking of set membership with a tunable balance between space usage and false positive rates.

Chapter 47

B-Tree and B+ Tree Data Structures

Below is a Python code snippet that explores the core operations of a B-tree, including insertion, search, and traversal functionalities.

```python
class BTreeNode:
    def __init__(self, leaf=False):
        self.leaf = leaf
        self.keys = []
        self.children = []

class BTree:
    def __init__(self, t):
        self.root = BTreeNode(True)
        self.t = t  # Minimum degree

    def insert(self, key):
        root = self.root
        if len(root.keys) == (2 * self.t) - 1:
            temp = BTreeNode()
            self.root = temp
            temp.children.insert(0, root)
            self.split_child(temp, 0)
            self.insert_non_full(temp, key)
        else:
            self.insert_non_full(root, key)

    def insert_non_full(self, node, key):
        i = len(node.keys) - 1
        if node.leaf:
            node.keys.append(0)
            while i >= 0 and key < node.keys[i]:
```

```
                    node.keys[i + 1] = node.keys[i]
                    i -= 1
                node.keys[i + 1] = key
        else:
            while i >= 0 and key < node.keys[i]:
                i -= 1
            i += 1
            if len(node.children[i].keys) == (2 * self.t) - 1:
                self.split_child(node, i)
                if key > node.keys[i]:
                    i += 1
            self.insert_non_full(node.children[i], key)

    def split_child(self, parent, index):
        t = self.t
        child = parent.children[index]
        new_child = BTreeNode(child.leaf)
        new_child.keys = child.keys[t:(2 * t) - 1]
        child.keys = child.keys[0:t - 1]
        if not child.leaf:
            new_child.children = child.children[t:(2 * t)]
            child.children = child.children[0:t]
        parent.children.insert(index + 1, new_child)
        parent.keys.insert(index, child.keys[t - 1])

    def search(self, k, node=None):
        if node is None:
            node = self.root
        i = 0
        while i < len(node.keys) and k > node.keys[i]:
            i += 1
        if i < len(node.keys) and k == node.keys[i]:
            return node, i
        elif node.leaf:
            return None
        else:
            return self.search(k, node.children[i])

    def traverse(self, node=None):
        if node is None:
            node = self.root
        for i in range(len(node.keys)):
            if not node.leaf:
                self.traverse(node.children[i])
            print(node.keys[i], end=" ")
        if not node.leaf:
            self.traverse(node.children[len(node.keys)])

# Example Usage
btree = BTree(3)
values = [10, 20, 5, 6, 12, 30, 7, 17]
for val in values:
    btree.insert(val)
```

```
print("Traversal of the constructed B-tree is:")
btree.traverse()
print()

search_key = 30
result = btree.search(search_key)
if result:
    print(f"Key {search_key} found in B-tree.")
else:
    print(f"Key {search_key} not found in B-tree.")
```

This code defines the essential components of a B-tree data structure:

- The **BTreeNode** class represents the node structure, including keys and children.

- The **insert** method handles the insertion operation by managing node fullness and ensuring keys are correctly placed.

- The **split_child** method helps maintain B-tree properties by splitting full child nodes.

- The **search** function checks for the presence of a key within the tree.

- The **traverse** method performs an in-order traversal, displaying all keys in ascending order.

This implementation demonstrates how B-trees manage data storage efficiently in databases and filesystems, offering balanced and organized node structures.

Chapter 48

Skip Lists: Concurrent and Lock-Free Implementations

Below is a Python code snippet that demonstrates the fundamental operations of concurrent skip lists, particularly emphasizing lock-free designs, thread safety, and synchronization in concurrent environments.

```python
import threading
import random

class Node:
    def __init__(self, key=None, height=1):
        self.key = key
        self.next = [None] * height

class SkipList:
    def __init__(self, max_height=16):
        self.head = Node(height=max_height)
        self.max_height = max_height
        self.size = 0
        self.lock = threading.Lock()

    def find(self, key):
        update = [None] * self.max_height
        current = self.head
        for level in range(self.max_height - 1, -1, -1):
            while current.next[level] and current.next[level].key < 
            ↪   key:
                current = current.next[level]
```

```
            update[level] = current
        return update

    def insert(self, key):
        with self.lock:
            update = self.find(key)
            current = update[0].next[0]
            if current and current.key == key:
                return False  # Key already exists

            new_height = self.random_height()
            new_node = Node(key, new_height)
            for level in range(new_height):
                new_node.next[level] = update[level].next[level]
                update[level].next[level] = new_node

            self.size += 1
            return True

    def delete(self, key):
        with self.lock:
            update = self.find(key)
            current = update[0].next[0]
            if not current or current.key != key:
                return False  # Key not found

            for level in range(self.max_height):
                if update[level].next[level] != current:
                    break
                update[level].next[level] = current.next[level]

            self.size -= 1
            return True

    def contains(self, key):
        update = self.find(key)
        current = update[0].next[0]
        return current and current.key == key

    def random_height(self):
        height = 1
        while height < self.max_height and random.random() < 0.5:
            height += 1
        return height

# Example usage:
skip_list = SkipList()

insert_threads = [threading.Thread(target=skip_list.insert,
↪ args=(i,)) for i in range(100)]
for thread in insert_threads:
    thread.start()
for thread in insert_threads:
```

```
    thread.join()

print("Size after inserts:", skip_list.size)

delete_threads = [threading.Thread(target=skip_list.delete,
→  args=(i,)) for i in range(50)]
for thread in delete_threads:
    thread.start()
for thread in delete_threads:
    thread.join()

print("Size after deletes:", skip_list.size)

print("Contains 25:", skip_list.contains(25))
print("Contains 75:", skip_list.contains(75))
```

This code demonstrates key aspects of designing thread-safe concurrent skip lists using lock mechanisms in Python:

- **Node** class defines the structure for each skip list node containing multi-level pointers.

- **SkipList** class provides core functionality, including **insert**, **delete**, and **contains** operations, protected by locks to ensure atomicity in concurrent environments.

- **find** and **random_height** are auxiliary methods supporting efficient skip list navigation and level determination.

- Example usage illustrates concurrent insertion and deletion, showcasing thread safety across multiple threads.

The structure ensures synchronization mechanisms are in place to accommodate concurrent access, thereby balancing performance and thread safety.

Chapter 49

Trie Data Structure and Its Variants

Below is a Python code snippet that demonstrates trie implementation including basic operations such as insertion, search, and deletion. Additionally, this code illustrates variations like compressed tries and radix trees for efficient retrieval and storage.

```python
class TrieNode:
    def __init__(self):
        self.children = {}
        self.is_end_of_word = False

class Trie:
    def __init__(self):
        self.root = TrieNode()

    def insert(self, word):
        """
        Insert a word into the trie.
        :param word: The word to be inserted.
        """
        node = self.root
        for char in word:
            if char not in node.children:
                node.children[char] = TrieNode()
            node = node.children[char]
        node.is_end_of_word = True

    def search(self, word):
        """
        Search for a word in the trie.
        :param word: The word to search for.
```

```python
        :return: True if the word is found, False otherwise.
        """
        node = self.root
        for char in word:
            if char not in node.children:
                return False
            node = node.children[char]
        return node.is_end_of_word

    def delete(self, word):
        """
        Delete a word from the trie.
        :param word: The word to be deleted.
        """
        def _delete(node, word, depth):
            if not node:
                return False

            if depth == len(word):
                if node.is_end_of_word:
                    node.is_end_of_word = False
                return len(node.children) == 0

            char = word[depth]
            if char in node.children:
                should_delete_child = _delete(node.children[char],
                ↪  word, depth + 1)
                if should_delete_child:
                    del node.children[char]
                    return not node.is_end_of_word and
                    ↪  len(node.children) == 0
            return False

        _delete(self.root, word, 0)


# Example usage:
trie = Trie()
trie.insert("hello")
trie.insert("helium")
print(trie.search("hello"))   # Output: True
print(trie.search("helium"))  # Output: True
print(trie.search("hi"))      # Output: False
trie.delete("hello")
print(trie.search("hello"))   # Output: False

# Radix Trie (Compressed Trie) Example Implementation
class RadixNode:
    def __init__(self, key):
        self.children = {}
        self.key = key
        self.is_end_of_word = False


class RadixTrie:
```

```python
def __init__(self):
    self.root = RadixNode("")

def insert(self, word):
    """
    Insert a word into the radix trie.
    :param word: The word to be inserted.
    """
    current = self.root
    i = 0

    while i < len(word):
        char = word[i]
        part = ""

        if char in current.children:
            part = current.children[char].key
            if word.startswith(part, i):
                current = current.children[char]
                i += len(part)
            else:
                common_prefix_length = \
                    self.common_prefix_length(part, word[i:])
                new_node = \
                    RadixNode(part[:common_prefix_length])
                current.children[char].key = \
                    part[common_prefix_length:]
                new_node.children[part[common_prefix_length]] = \
                    current.children[char]
                current.children[char] = new_node
                current = new_node
                i += common_prefix_length
        else:
            current.children[char] = RadixNode(word[i:])
            current = current.children[char]
            break

    current.is_end_of_word = True

def common_prefix_length(self, str1, str2):
    """
    Find the common prefix length between two strings.
    :param str1: First string.
    :param str2: Second string.
    :return: Length of the common prefix.
    """
    length = 0
    for x, y in zip(str1, str2):
        if x == y:
            length += 1
        else:
            break
    return length
```

```
def search(self, word):
    """
    Search for a word in the radix trie.
    :param word: The word to search for.
    :return: True if the word is found, False otherwise.
    """
    current = self.root
    i = 0

    while i < len(word):
        char = word[i]
        if char in current.children:
            part = current.children[char].key
            if word.startswith(part, i):
                current = current.children[char]
                i += len(part)
            else:
                return False
        else:
            return False

    return current.is_end_of_word

# Example usage:
radix_trie = RadixTrie()
radix_trie.insert("hello")
radix_trie.insert("helium")
print(radix_trie.search("hello"))   # Output: True
print(radix_trie.search("helium"))  # Output: True
print(radix_trie.search("hi"))      # Output: False
```

This code provides a basic 'Trie' implementation along with a compressed version known as 'Radix Trie' or compressed trie. Key operations include:

- **insert**: Adds a new word to the trie, creating nodes as necessary.

- **search**: Checks for the existence of a word in the trie.

- **delete**: Removes a word from the trie by eliminating its terminal representation.

- In 'Radix Trie', the `common_prefix_length` function is used to find common prefixes, enhancing the compression of the trie structure.

The code also contains usage examples demonstrating insertion, searching, and deletion operations in both `Trie` and `RadixTrie`.

Chapter 50

Suffix Tries and Suffix Automata

Below is a Python code snippet that demonstrates the construction of a suffix trie, including a class for trie nodes, the trie itself, and methods for insertion and search functionalities.

```python
class TrieNode:
    def __init__(self):
        self.children = {}
        self.is_end_of_word = False

class SuffixTrie:
    def __init__(self, text):
        self.root = TrieNode()
        self._build_suffix_trie(text)

    def _insert_suffix(self, suffix):
        current = self.root
        for char in suffix:
            if char not in current.children:
                current.children[char] = TrieNode()
            current = current.children[char]
        current.is_end_of_word = True

    def _build_suffix_trie(self, text):
        for i in range(len(text)):
            suffix = text[i:]
            self._insert_suffix(suffix)

    def search(self, pattern):
        current = self.root
        for char in pattern:
```

```python
            if char not in current.children:
                return False
            current = current.children[char]
        return True

# Example usage
text = "bananas"
pattern_to_search = "ana"

# Create a suffix trie
suffix_trie = SuffixTrie(text)

# Search for a pattern
is_present = suffix_trie.search(pattern_to_search)
print(f"'{pattern_to_search}' found in '{text}': {is_present}")
```

This Python code provides a simple implementation of a suffix trie:

- `TrieNode` class represents a node in the trie structure, storing children nodes and a boolean for end of word markers.

- `SuffixTrie` class builds the suffix trie from a given text, providing methods to insert suffixes and search for patterns.

- `_insert_suffix` is a private method that inserts each suffix of the text into the trie.

- `_build_suffix_trie` constructs the entire trie by iterating through possible suffixes.

- `search` method checks if a given pattern exists within the constructed trie, validating the structure's capability.

The final code block constructs a suffix trie from the input string `text` and demonstrates searching for a pattern within this structure.

Chapter 51

Quad Trees and Octrees in Spatial Indexing

Below is a Python code snippet that encompasses the core computational elements of the quad tree and octree data structures, including their construction, insertion, and query operations tailored for spatial partitioning:

```python
class QuadTree:
    def __init__(self, boundary, capacity):
        self.boundary = boundary    # boundary should be a Rectangle
        self.capacity = capacity    # capacity of the quadtree node
        self.points = []
        self.divided = False

    def subdivide(self):
        x, y = self.boundary.x, self.boundary.y
        w, h = self.boundary.w / 2, self.boundary.h / 2

        ne = Rectangle(x + w, y - h, w, h)
        nw = Rectangle(x - w, y - h, w, h)
        se = Rectangle(x + w, y + h, w, h)
        sw = Rectangle(x - w, y + h, w, h)

        self.northeast = QuadTree(ne, self.capacity)
        self.northwest = QuadTree(nw, self.capacity)
        self.southeast = QuadTree(se, self.capacity)
        self.southwest = QuadTree(sw, self.capacity)
        self.divided = True
```

```python
    def insert(self, point):
        if not self.boundary.contains(point):
            return False

        if len(self.points) < self.capacity:
            self.points.append(point)
            return True
        else:
            if not self.divided:
                self.subdivide()

            if self.northeast.insert(point):
                return True
            if self.northwest.insert(point):
                return True
            if self.southeast.insert(point):
                return True
            if self.southwest.insert(point):
                return True

    def query(self, range, found):
        if not self.boundary.intersects(range):
            return
        else:
            for p in self.points:
                if range.contains(p):
                    found.append(p)

            if self.divided:
                self.northwest.query(range, found)
                self.northeast.query(range, found)
                self.southwest.query(range, found)
                self.southeast.query(range, found)

# Rectangle class representing the boundary
class Rectangle:
    def __init__(self, x, y, w, h):
        self.x = x
        self.y = y
        self.w = w
        self.h = h

    def contains(self, point):
        return (point.x >= self.x - self.w and
                point.x < self.x + self.w and
                point.y >= self.y - self.h and
                point.y < self.y + self.h)

    def intersects(self, range):
        return not (range.x - range.w > self.x + self.w or
                    range.x + range.w < self.x - self.w or
                    range.y - range.h > self.y + self.h or
                    range.y + range.h < self.y - self.h)
```

```
# Point class
class Point:
    def __init__(self, x, y):
        self.x = x
        self.y = y

# Octree and other implementations follow similarly in three
↪    dimensions
```

This code defines several key elements necessary for implementing quad trees and octrees:

- **QuadTree** class manages the structure of the spatial partition, allowing for efficient querying and point insertion.

- **subdivide** method subdivides a node into four children when the capacity is exceeded, crucial for adapting the quadtree dynamically.

- **insert** method handles the placement of points within the tree structure, ensuring spatial data is efficiently organized.

- **query** method performs range searches, retrieving points within a specified area, which is vital for applications like collision detection and geographic information systems.

- **Rectangle** and **Point** classes provide fundamental geometric operations to interface with the quadtree structure.

The final implementation shows how to organize spatial data using quad trees, highlighting its capabilities in efficient spatial queries and subdivisions.

Chapter 52

Red-Black Tree: A Self-Balancing Binary Search Tree

Below is a Python code snippet that encompasses the core computational elements of red-black tree operations including insertion, deletion, and balancing.

```python
class Node:
    def __init__(self, data):
        self.data = data
        self.color = "RED"
        self.left = None
        self.right = None
        self.parent = None

class RedBlackTree:
    def __init__(self):
        self.TNULL = Node(0)
        self.TNULL.color = "BLACK"
        self.root = self.TNULL

    def left_rotate(self, x):
        y = x.right
        x.right = y.left
        if y.left != self.TNULL:
            y.left.parent = x

        y.parent = x.parent
        if x.parent is None:
            self.root = y
```

```
        elif x == x.parent.left:
            x.parent.left = y
        else:
            x.parent.right = y
        y.left = x
        x.parent = y

    def right_rotate(self, y):
        x = y.left
        y.left = x.right
        if x.right != self.TNULL:
            x.right.parent = y

        x.parent = y.parent
        if y.parent is None:
            self.root = x
        elif y == y.parent.right:
            y.parent.right = x
        else:
            y.parent.left = x
        x.right = y
        y.parent = x

    def insert_fixup(self, k):
        while k.parent.color == "RED":
            if k.parent == k.parent.parent.right:
                u = k.parent.parent.left
                if u.color == "RED":
                    u.color = "BLACK"
                    k.parent.color = "BLACK"
                    k.parent.parent.color = "RED"
                    k = k.parent.parent
                else:
                    if k == k.parent.left:
                        k = k.parent
                        self.right_rotate(k)
                    k.parent.color = "BLACK"
                    k.parent.parent.color = "RED"
                    self.left_rotate(k.parent.parent)
            else:
                u = k.parent.parent.right
                if u.color == "RED":
                    u.color = "BLACK"
                    k.parent.color = "BLACK"
                    k.parent.parent.color = "RED"
                    k = k.parent.parent
                else:
                    if k == k.parent.right:
                        k = k.parent
                        self.left_rotate(k)
                    k.parent.color = "BLACK"
                    k.parent.parent.color = "RED"
                    self.right_rotate(k.parent.parent)
```

```python
            if k == self.root:
                break
        self.root.color = "BLACK"

    def insert(self, key):
        node = Node(key)
        node.parent = None
        node.data = key
        node.left = self.TNULL
        node.right = self.TNULL
        node.color = "RED"

        y = None
        x = self.root

        while x != self.TNULL:
            y = x
            if node.data < x.data:
                x = x.left
            else:
                x = x.right

        node.parent = y
        if y is None:
            self.root = node
        elif node.data < y.data:
            y.left = node
        else:
            y.right = node

        if node.parent is None:
            node.color = "BLACK"
            return

        if node.parent.parent is None:
            return

        self.insert_fixup(node)

    def get_root(self):
        return self.root

    def __inorder_helper(self, node):
        if node != self.TNULL:
            self.__inorder_helper(node.left)
            print(node.data)
            self.__inorder_helper(node.right)

    def inorder(self):
        self.__inorder_helper(self.root)

    def __preorder_helper(self, node):
        if node != self.TNULL:
```

```
            print(node.data)
            self.__preorder_helper(node.left)
            self.__preorder_helper(node.right)

    def preorder(self):
        self.__preorder_helper(self.root)

    def __postorder_helper(self, node):
        if node != self.TNULL:
            self.__postorder_helper(node.left)
            self.__postorder_helper(node.right)
            print(node.data)

    def postorder(self):
        self.__postorder_helper(self.root)

# Example use of RedBlackTree
rbt = RedBlackTree()
rbt.insert(20)
rbt.insert(15)
rbt.insert(25)
rbt.insert(10)
rbt.insert(5)

print("Inorder Traversal: ")
rbt.inorder()
```

This code defines several key functions necessary for the implementation and management of red-black trees:

- `left_rotate` and `right_rotate` functions perform the rotations necessary to maintain the tree balance.

- `insert_fixup` ensures that the red-black tree properties are restored after insertion.

- `insert` adds a new node to the red-black tree while ensuring compliance with structural properties.

- Traversal methods `inorder`, `preorder`, and `postorder` provide different methods of visiting nodes.

The final block demonstrates how to use the red-black tree for basic insertions and inorder traversal.

Chapter 53

AVL Trees: Height-Balanced Binary Search Trees

Below is a Python code snippet implementing an AVL tree that maintains strict balance conditions through rotation operations during insertion and deletion.

```python
class AVLNode:
    def __init__(self, key, height=1, left=None, right=None):
        self.key = key
        self.height = height
        self.left = left
        self.right = right

class AVLTree:
    def insert(self, root, key):
        # Perform normal BST insert
        if root is None:
            return AVLNode(key)

        if key < root.key:
            root.left = self.insert(root.left, key)
        else:
            root.right = self.insert(root.right, key)

        # Update the height
        root.height = 1 + max(self.get_height(root.left),
        ↪    self.get_height(root.right))

        # Get the balance factor
```

```python
        balance = self.get_balance(root)

        # If the node is unbalanced, then there are 4 cases

        # Left Left Case
        if balance > 1 and key < root.left.key:
            return self.right_rotate(root)

        # Right Right Case
        if balance < -1 and key > root.right.key:
            return self.left_rotate(root)

        # Left Right Case
        if balance > 1 and key > root.left.key:
            root.left = self.left_rotate(root.left)
            return self.right_rotate(root)

        # Right Left Case
        if balance < -1 and key < root.right.key:
            root.right = self.right_rotate(root.right)
            return self.left_rotate(root)

        return root

    def delete(self, root, key):
        # Perform standard BST delete
        if root is None:
            return root

        if key < root.key:
            root.left = self.delete(root.left, key)
        elif key > root.key:
            root.right = self.delete(root.right, key)
        else:
            if root.left is None:
                temp = root.right
                root = None
                return temp

            elif root.right is None:
                temp = root.left
                root = None
                return temp

            temp = self.get_min_value_node(root.right)
            root.key = temp.key
            root.right = self.delete(root.right, temp.key)

        if root is None:
            return root

        # Update the height
```

```python
        root.height = 1 + max(self.get_height(root.left),
        ↪    self.get_height(root.right))

        # Get the balance factor
        balance = self.get_balance(root)

        # Balance the tree

        # Left Left Case
        if balance > 1 and self.get_balance(root.left) >= 0:
            return self.right_rotate(root)

        # Left Right Case
        if balance > 1 and self.get_balance(root.left) < 0:
            root.left = self.left_rotate(root.left)
            return self.right_rotate(root)

        # Right Right Case
        if balance < -1 and self.get_balance(root.right) <= 0:
            return self.left_rotate(root)

        # Right Left Case
        if balance < -1 and self.get_balance(root.right) > 0:
            root.right = self.right_rotate(root.right)
            return self.left_rotate(root)

        return root

    def left_rotate(self, z):
        y = z.right
        T2 = y.left

        y.left = z
        z.right = T2

        z.height = 1 + max(self.get_height(z.left),
        ↪    self.get_height(z.right))
        y.height = 1 + max(self.get_height(y.left),
        ↪    self.get_height(y.right))

        return y

    def right_rotate(self, y):
        x = y.left
        T2 = x.right

        x.right = y
        y.left = T2

        y.height = 1 + max(self.get_height(y.left),
        ↪    self.get_height(y.right))
        x.height = 1 + max(self.get_height(x.left),
        ↪    self.get_height(x.right))
```

167

```
        return x

    def get_height(self, node):
        if not node:
            return 0
        return node.height

    def get_balance(self, node):
        if not node:
            return 0
        return self.get_height(node.left) -
        ↪   self.get_height(node.right)

    def get_min_value_node(self, node):
        if node is None or node.left is None:
            return node
        return self.get_min_value_node(node.left)

    def pre_order(self, root):
        if not root:
            return
        print(root.key, end=' ')
        self.pre_order(root.left)
        self.pre_order(root.right)

# Example Usage:
avl_tree = AVLTree()
root = None

keys = [10, 20, 30, 40, 50, 25]

for key in keys:
    root = avl_tree.insert(root, key)

# Preorder traversal of the constructed AVL tree
print("Preorder traversal of the AVL tree:")
avl_tree.pre_order(root)

# Delete a key and show preorder traversal
root = avl_tree.delete(root, 10)
print("\nPreorder traversal after deletion of 10:")
avl_tree.pre_order(root)
```

This code defines the essential operations for an AVL Tree, including insertion and deletion, while maintaining balance through rotations:

- **insert** adds elements while ensuring the tree remains balanced through rotations.

168

- **delete** removes elements, restructuring the tree to preserve AVL balance, employing appropriate rotations.

- **left_rotate** and **right_rotate** perform essential rotations to maintain tree balance.

- **get_height** and **get_balance** functions help manage AVL tree invariants related to height.

- **pre_order** offers a method to traverse the tree in preorder to verify tree structure.

The final segment of code demonstrates how the AVL tree's insertion and deletion maintain strict balance, showing preorder traversal outputs before and after a deletion operation.

Chapter 54

MapReduce Algorithm for Big Data Processing

Below is a Python code snippet illustrating the **MapReduce** programming model used for processing large data sets in parallel using distributed algorithms. This example includes the implementation of **map** and **reduce** functions to perform a simple word count operation over a set of documents.

```
from collections import defaultdict

def map_function(document):
    '''
    Map function that takes a document and emits key-value pairs of
    ↪   word and count.
    :param document: A string or text document.
    :return: List of tuples (word, 1) for each word in the document.
    '''
    # Split the document into words
    words = document.split()
    # Emit a count of 1 for each word
    return [(word.lower(), 1) for word in words]

def reduce_function(word, counts):
    '''
    Reduce function that aggregates counts for each word, given the
    ↪   intermediate list.
    :param word: A single word.
    :param counts: A list of tuples representing counts from
    ↪   different mappers.
```

```
        :return: A tuple (word, total_count) for the word.
        '''
        # Aggregate counts for the current word
        total_count = sum(counts)
        return (word, total_count)

def execute_map_reduce(documents):
        '''
        Combines map and reduce functions to perform a complete
        ↪    MapReduce operation.
        :param documents: A list of text documents.
        :return: A dictionary with words as keys and their total counts
        ↪    as values.
        '''
        # An intermediate map result holder
        intermediate = defaultdict(list)

        # Map phase
        for document in documents:
            for word, count in map_function(document):
                intermediate[word].append(count)

        # Reduce phase
        results = {}
        for word, counts in intermediate.items():
            results[word] = reduce_function(word, counts)

        return results

# Sample run
documents = [
    "MapReduce is a programming model",
    "It is a framework for processing large data sets with a
    ↪    distributed algorithm",
    "Key components are map function and reduce function"
]

# Execute the MapReduce operation
word_counts = execute_map_reduce(documents)
print("Word counts:", word_counts)
```

This code defines and executes key functions involved in the
MapReduce model:

- The `map_function` processes individual documents, emitting
  intermediate key-value pairs (word, count).

- The `reduce_function` aggregates the counts from the map
  phase across all inputs for each word.

- `execute_map_reduce` orchestrates the overall process, combining the map and reduce functions to produce a final word

171

count across multiple documents.

The implemented example demonstrates a word-counting use case with three simple text documents, showcasing the `MapReduce` paradigm's capability to handle parallel and distributed data processing.

Chapter 55

Bulk Synchronous Parallel (BSP) Model

Below is a Python code snippet that demonstrates the implementation of the Bulk Synchronous Parallel (BSP) model, highlighting aspects like computation, communication, and synchronization in a parallel processing environment.

```python
import threading
import time
from queue import Queue

class BSPNode:
    def __init__(self, node_id, total_nodes, local_computation,
    ↪ exchange_data):
        '''
        Initialize a BSP Node.
        :param node_id: Unique identifier for the node.
        :param total_nodes: Total number of nodes in the system.
        :param local_computation: Function representing local
        ↪ computation task.
        :param exchange_data: Function to handle data exchange
        ↪ between nodes.
        '''
        self.node_id = node_id
        self.total_nodes = total_nodes
        self.local_computation = local_computation
        self.exchange_data = exchange_data
        self.inbox = Queue()
        self.outbox = {i: None for i in range(total_nodes)}

    def send_data(self, data, to_node):
```

173

```
        '''
        Simulate sending data to another node.
        :param data: Data to be sent.
        :param to_node: ID of the receiving node.
        '''
        self.outbox[to_node] = data

    def receive_data(self, from_node):
        '''
        Simulate receiving data from another node.
        :param from_node: ID of the sending node.
        :return: Received data.
        '''
        return self.inbox.get(from_node, None)

    def perform_computation(self):
        '''
        Perform local computation and prepare data for
        ↪   communication.
        '''
        local_result = self.local_computation(self.node_id)
        for neighbor_id in range(self.total_nodes):
            if neighbor_id != self.node_id:
                self.send_data(f"Data from {self.node_id}",
                ↪   neighbor_id)
        return local_result

    def synchronize(self):
        '''
        Simulate synchronization step where data is exchanged
        ↪   between nodes.
        '''
        for to_node, data in self.outbox.items():
            if data is not None:
                # In practice, this would involve network
                ↪   communication
                nodes[to_node].inbox.put(data)

def example_local_computation(node_id):
    '''
    Example function for local computation.
    :param node_id: ID of the node performing the computation.
    :return: Computation result.
    '''
    print(f"Node {node_id} performing local computation.")
    time.sleep(1)   # simulate computation delay
    return f"Result from Node {node_id}"

def example_exchange_data(node, data):
    '''
    Example function to handle data exchange.
    :param node: Current node instance.
    :param data: Data to process.
```

174

```
        ' ' '
        print(f"Node {node.node_id} processing {data}")

# Setup the BSP system
total_nodes = 4
nodes = [BSPNode(node_id=i, total_nodes=total_nodes,
                 local_computation=example_local_computation,
                 exchange_data=example_exchange_data) for i in
            ↪    range(total_nodes)]

def node_task(node):
    # Execute local computation
    local_result = node.perform_computation()

    # Synchronize with other nodes
    node.synchronize()

    # Process received data
    while not node.inbox.empty():
        received_data = node.inbox.get()
        node.exchange_data(node, received_data)

# Run each node in a separate thread to simulate parallel execution
threads = [threading.Thread(target=node_task, args=(node,)) for node
    ↪  in nodes]

# Start all threads
for thread in threads:
    thread.start()

# Wait for all threads to complete
for thread in threads:
    thread.join()
```

This code defines several key components essential for implementing a Bulk Synchronous Parallel (BSP) model:

- The BSPNode class represents each processing unit, handling local computations, data sending, and receiving.

- perform_computation encapsulates the local computational task performed by a node.

- synchronize allows nodes to exchange data, mimicking network communication through queues.

- example_local_computation and example_exchange_data are illustrative examples demonstrating local computational tasks and data processing, respectively.

- Parallelism is achieved by using Python's threading to simulate each node's operation.

This setup allows for demonstration and exploration of computation, communication, and synchronization complexities inherent to parallel processing models like BSP.

Chapter 56

Parallel Sorting Algorithms: Bitonic Sort and More

Below is a Python code snippet that implements parallel sorting algorithms such as Bitonic Sort and Odd-Even Mergesort, designed for multi-processor systems, demonstrating core parallel computation features in Python.

```python
import multiprocessing
import numpy as np

def bitonic_sort(arr, up=True):
    '''
    Perform bitonic sort on the given array.
    :param arr: Array to be sorted.
    :param up: Boolean to choose the sorting order.
    '''
    length = len(arr)
    if length <= 1:
        return arr

    first_half = bitonic_sort(arr[:length // 2], True)
    second_half = bitonic_sort(arr[length // 2:], False)
    return bitonic_merge(first_half + second_half, up)

def bitonic_merge(arr, up):
    '''
    Perform bitonic merge on the array.
    :param arr: Array to be merged.
    :param up: Boolean to choose the merging direction.
```

```python
    '''
    length = len(arr)
    if length == 1:
        return arr

    for i in range(length // 2):
        if (arr[i] > arr[i + length // 2]) == up:
            arr[i], arr[i + length // 2] = arr[i + length // 2],
            ↪   arr[i]

    first_half = bitonic_merge(arr[:length // 2], up)
    second_half = bitonic_merge(arr[length // 2:], up)
    return first_half + second_half

def odd_even_mergesort(arr):
    '''
    Perform Odd-Even Mergesort on the array.
    :param arr: Array to be sorted.
    '''
    if len(arr) <= 1:
        return arr

    mid = len(arr) // 2
    left = odd_even_mergesort(arr[:mid])
    right = odd_even_mergesort(arr[mid:])
    return odd_even_merge(left + right)

def odd_even_merge(arr):
    '''
    Perform Odd-Even merge on the array.
    :param arr: Array to be merged.
    '''
    if len(arr) == 1:
        return arr

    even = arr[::2]
    odd = arr[1::2]
    even_sorted = odd_even_merge(even)
    odd_sorted = odd_even_merge(odd)

    combined = []
    for i in range(len(arr)//2):
        combined.append(even_sorted[i])
        if i < len(odd_sorted):
            combined.append(odd_sorted[i])

    return combined

def parallel_bitonic_sort(arr):
    '''
    Perform parallel Bitonic sort.
    :param arr: Array to be sorted.
    '''
```

```python
pool = multiprocessing.Pool()
size = len(arr)
sorted_arr = pool.starmap(bitonic_sort, [(arr[i:i + size], True)
                    for i in range(0, len(arr), size)])
pool.close()
return bitonic_merge(np.concatenate(sorted_arr), True)

# Example usage
data = np.random.rand(16)  # replace with large data for realistic
↪   computation
sorted_data = parallel_bitonic_sort(data)
print("Sorted data:", sorted_data)
```

This code snippet details the implementation of Bitonic Sort and Odd-Even Mergesort alongside a parallel version of Bitonic Sort using Python's multiprocessing capabilities:

- `bitonic_sort` is implemented to recursively sort an array into a bitonic sequence.

- `bitonic_merge` takes a bitonic sequence and orders it fully.

- `odd_even_mergesort` sorts an array using a recursive approach, leveraging odd-even merging.

- `odd_even_merge` responsibly merges arrays produced by odd-even mergesort.

- `parallel_bitonic_sort` demonstrates a simple parallelization of bitonic sort utilizing Python's multiprocessing capabilities, highlighting the separation of tasks and remerging.

These functions work synergistically to perform efficient sorting suitable for multi-processor systems.

Chapter 57

Fast Fourier Transform (FFT) Algorithm

Below is a Python code snippet that demonstrates the implementation of the Fast Fourier Transform (FFT) using the Cooley-Tukey algorithm for efficient computation of discrete Fourier transforms. It includes the core recursive function and demonstrates the radix-2 decimation-in-time approach.

```python
import numpy as np

def fft(x):
    '''
    Compute the FFT of an array using the radix-2 Cooley-Tukey
    ↪ algorithm.
    :param x: Input array of complex numbers (length must be a power
    ↪ of 2).
    :return: Array of the same length representing the FFT.
    '''
    N = len(x)
    if N <= 1:
        return x

    even = fft(x[::2])
    odd = fft(x[1::2])

    t = [np.exp(-2j * np.pi * k / N) * odd[k] for k in range(N //
    ↪ 2)]
    return [even[k] + t[k] for k in range(N // 2)] + [even[k] - t[k]
    ↪ for k in range(N // 2)]

# Example input
```

```
x = np.random.random(8) + 1j*np.random.random(8)    # Random complex
↪    array of power 2 length
# Perform FFT
X = fft(x)

print("Input array:", x)
print("FFT of the input array:", X)
```

This code defines the main function for computing the discrete Fourier transform using the FFT:

- The function `fft` is implemented recursively, dividing the input into even and odd indexed arrays, and computing the FFT of each.

- The exponential factors, known as twiddle factors, are computed and used to combine the results from the recursive calls.

- This implementation demonstrates the radix-2 decimation-in-time process, which requires the input array length to be a power of 2.

- An example input array of random complex numbers is provided to demonstrate the FFT computation and output.

The final block of code prints the input array and its FFT, showcasing this powerful computation method in practice.

Chapter 58

Conjugate Gradient Method for Solving Linear Systems

Below is a Python code snippet that demonstrates the implementation of the conjugate gradient algorithm for solving large, sparse, symmetric positive-definite linear systems. The code includes the definition of the algorithm and its application to a simple linear system.

```python
import numpy as np

def conj_grad(A, b, x0=None, tol=1e-10, max_iter=1000):
    '''
    Solve a linear system Ax = b using the Conjugate Gradient (CG)
    ↪   method.

    :param A: Symmetric positive-definite matrix.
    :param b: Right-hand side vector.
    :param x0: Initial guess for the solution.
    :param tol: Tolerance for convergence.
    :param max_iter: Maximum number of iterations.
    :return: Solution vector x.
    '''
    n = b.shape[0]
    if x0 is None:
        x0 = np.zeros(n)

    x = x0
    r = b - np.dot(A, x)
```

```
        p = r.copy()
        rsold = np.dot(r, r)

        for i in range(max_iter):
            Ap = np.dot(A, p)
            alpha = rsold / np.dot(p, Ap)
            x += alpha * p
            r -= alpha * Ap
            rsnew = np.dot(r, r)

            if np.sqrt(rsnew) < tol:
                print(f"Convergence reached after {i+1} iterations.")
                break

            p = r + (rsnew / rsold) * p
            rsold = rsnew

        return x

# Example usage:

# Define a symmetric positive-definite matrix A and a vector b
A = np.array([[4.0, 1.0, 0.0],
              [1.0, 3.0, 1.0],
              [0.0, 1.0, 2.0]])

b = np.array([1.0, 2.0, 3.0])

# Solve Ax = b using the conjugate gradient method
x0 = np.array([0.0, 0.0, 0.0])   # Initial guess
solution = conj_grad(A, b, x0)

print("Solution:", solution)
```

This code defines several key functions necessary for the implementation of the conjugate gradient algorithm:

- `conj_grad` function solves the linear system using the conjugate gradient method, taking into account the symmetric positive-definiteness of the matrix.

- The function iteratively updates the solution vector by optimizing the direction of descent, achieving convergence within the specified tolerance.

- An example demonstrates how to set up a symmetric positive-definite matrix and vector, then solve the linear system using the conjugate gradient method.

The example block of code provides a basic application of the algorithm to illustrate how it operates on a simple linear system.

183

Chapter 59

Newton-Raphson Method for Root Finding

Below is a Python code snippet using the **Newton-Raphson** method to find successively better approximations to the roots of a real-valued function.

```python
import numpy as np

def newton_raphson(f, df, x0, epsilon=1e-6, max_iter=1000):
    '''
    Newton-Raphson method for finding roots of a real-valued
    ↪   function.
    :param f: Function for which the root is sought.
    :param df: Derivative of the function f.
    :param x0: Initial guess for the root.
    :param epsilon: Convergence tolerance.
    :param max_iter: Maximum number of iterations.
    :return: Estimated root.
    '''
    x = x0
    for i in range(max_iter):
        fx = f(x)
        dfx = df(x)

        if dfx == 0:
            print(f"Derivative zero at iteration {i}. No solution
            ↪   found.")
            return None
```

```python
    # Newton-Raphson iteration step
    x_new = x - fx / dfx

    # Check for convergence
    if abs(x_new - x) < epsilon:
        print(f"Converged to {x_new} after {i+1} iterations.")
        return x_new

    x = x_new

  print("Max iterations reached. No solution found.")
  return None

# Example usage
def func(x):
    return x**2 - 2

def der_func(x):
    return 2*x

# Initial guess
initial_guess = 1.0

# Finding the root using Newton-Raphson method
root = newton_raphson(func, der_func, initial_guess)

print("Estimated Root:", root)
```

This code snippet represents the core computational elements of the Newton-Raphson iterative method:

- `newton_raphson` function performs the iterative algorithm for root finding. It requires a function `f` whose root is desired, its derivative `df`, an initial guess `x0`, and optional parameters for tolerance and maximum iterations.

- Implements a loop that iterates up to `max_iter` times, updating the estimate of the root using the Newton-Raphson formula: $x\_new = x - \frac{f(x)}{f'(x)}$.

- Checks for convergence by comparing the absolute difference between successive estimates to a specified `epsilon`. If convergence is achieved, it prints a message with the iteration count and returns the root.

- Provides a sample function `func` and its derivative `der_func` to demonstrate finding the square root of 2 starting from the initial guess 1.0.

185

The final block outputs either the estimated root if the procedure converges or a message indicating failure otherwise.

Chapter 60

Christofides Algorithm for the Traveling Salesman Problem

Below is a Python code snippet that implements the Christofides algorithm for approximating a solution to the Traveling Salesman Problem (TSP). The code focuses on constructing a minimum spanning tree (MST), finding a minimum weight perfect matching, and generating an Eulerian circuit to provide a near-optimal tour.

```python
import networkx as nx
import itertools

def minimum_spanning_tree(graph):
    '''
    Compute the Minimum Spanning Tree (MST) of a graph using
    ↪ Kruskal's algorithm.
    :param graph: A NetworkX graph.
    :return: A new graph representing the MST.
    '''
    mst = nx.Graph()
    # Sort edges by weight
    sorted_edges = sorted(graph.edges(data=True), key=lambda edge:
    ↪ edge[2]['weight'])
    # A dictionary to find and union sets
    parent = dict()
    rank = dict()

    def find(v):
        if parent[v] != v:
```

```
                parent[v] = find(parent[v])
            return parent[v]

        def union(v1, v2):
            root1 = find(v1)
            root2 = find(v2)
            if root1 != root2:
                if rank[root1] > rank[root2]:
                    parent[root2] = root1
                else:
                    parent[root1] = root2
                    if rank[root1] == rank[root2]:
                        rank[root2] += 1

        for node in graph.nodes:
            parent[node] = node
            rank[node] = 0

        for u, v, data in sorted_edges:
            if find(u) != find(v):
                union(u, v)
                mst.add_edge(u, v, weight=data['weight'])

        return mst

    def minimum_weight_perfect_matching(odd_degree_nodes, graph):
        '''
        Find a minimum weight perfect matching for nodes with odd
        ↪ degrees.
        :param odd_degree_nodes: List of nodes with odd degree.
        :param graph: Original graph.
        :return: List of tuples representing the matching edges.
        '''
        odd_graph = graph.subgraph(odd_degree_nodes).copy()
        for u, v, data in odd_graph.edges(data=True):
            if 'weight' not in data:
                data['weight'] = graph[u][v]['weight']

        # Use maximum matching and its complement to find minimum weight
        ↪ matching
        matching = list(nx.max_weight_matching(odd_graph,
        ↪ maxcardinality=True))
        return matching

    def christofides_tsp(graph):
        '''
        Christofides algorithm to approximate the solution for the TSP.
        :param graph: A complete weighted graph.
        :return: A list representing the TSP tour.
        '''
        # Step 1: Create MST
        mst = minimum_spanning_tree(graph)
```

```python
# Step 2: Find nodes of odd degree in the MST
odd_degree_nodes = [node for node in mst.nodes() if
↪    mst.degree(node) % 2 == 1]

# Step 3: Find a minimum weight perfect matching
matching = minimum_weight_perfect_matching(odd_degree_nodes,
↪    graph)

# Step 4: Combine MST and matching to form an Eulerian
↪    multigraph
multi_graph = nx.MultiGraph(mst)
multi_graph.add_edges_from(matching)

# Step 5: Find an Eulerian tour in the multigraph
eulerian_circuit = list(nx.eulerian_circuit(multi_graph))

# Step 6: Make the tour Hamiltonian by shortcutting repeated
↪    vertices
visited = set()
tsp_tour = []
for u, v in eulerian_circuit:
    if u not in visited:
        tsp_tour.append(u)
        visited.add(u)
tsp_tour.append(tsp_tour[0])  # Return to the starting node

return tsp_tour

# Example usage:
G = nx.complete_graph(6)
positions = {0:(0,0), 1:(1,1), 2:(2,0), 3:(3,1), 4:(0,2), 5:(2,3)}
for i, j in itertools.combinations(G.nodes(), 2):
    G[i][j]['weight'] = int(nx.euclidean_distance(positions[i],
↪    positions[j]))

tour = christofides_tsp(G)
print("Christofides TSP Tour:", tour)
```

This code defines several key functions necessary for Christofides algorithm implementation:

- **minimum_spanning_tree** uses Kruskal's algorithm to compute the MST of a graph ensuring a foundation for the matching process.

- **minimum_weight_perfect_matching** finds the perfect matching among nodes of odd degree, minimizing the overall weight to achieve even degree nodes suitable for Eulerian path finding.

- `christofides_tsp` incorporates both MST and matching results to build an Eulerian circuit, which is then converted into a Hamiltonian circuit by eliminating repeated nodes in the Eulerian path.

The final section includes an example demonstrating how to create and solve a simple instance of the TSP using the Christofides algorithm on a complete graph.

Chapter 61

Polynomial-Time Approximation Schemes (PTAS)

Below is a Python code snippet that demonstrates a basic implementation framework for a **Polynomial-Time Approximation Scheme (PTAS)** using a simple optimization problem, such as the Subset Sum problem. The implementation showcases the balance between computational complexity and approximation accuracy.

```python
import itertools

def ptas_subset_sum(nums, target, epsilon):
    '''
    Polynomial-Time Approximation Scheme for the Subset Sum problem.
    :param nums: list of integers representing the set.
    :param target: target sum to approximate.
    :param epsilon: tolerance level for approximating target.
    :return: nearest subset meeting the criteria.
    '''
    n = len(nums)
    k = int(epsilon * n)   # number of elements allowed in
    ↪    approximation
    best_sum = 0
    best_subset = []

    # Iterate over all possible subset sizes up to k
    for size in range(1, k + 1):
        for subset in itertools.combinations(nums, size):
            current_sum = sum(subset)
```

```
            # Check if current subset sum is closer to the target
            if best_sum < current_sum <= target:
                best_sum = current_sum
                best_subset = subset

    return best_subset, best_sum

# Example application and output
nums = [3, 34, 4, 12, 5, 2]
target = 10
epsilon = 0.5

approximated_subset, approximated_sum = ptas_subset_sum(nums,
↪   target, epsilon)

print("Approximated Subset:", approximated_subset)
print("Approximated Sum:", approximated_sum)
```

In this code, the following components are considered:

- The function **ptas_subset_sum** is central to the PTAS implementation, where it accepts a list of numbers, a target, and an epsilon that defines how much solution cost we can afford versus the optimal.

- The function explores all possible combinations of numbers up to a size defined by **epsilon * n**, thus controlling the trade-off between accuracy and speed.

- **best_sum** and **best_subset** store the current best approximation to the target sum that can be achieved by subsets of the array.

The final example invocation of the code demonstrates how an approximate solution to the Subset Sum problem can be obtained within a user-defined tolerance, offering insights into PTAS operation for various optimization contexts.

Chapter 62

Minimax Algorithm in Game Theory

Below is a Python code snippet that demonstrates a basic implementation of the **minimax** algorithm, which is used in decision-making for zero-sum games like Tic-Tac-Toe. It features how the algorithm evaluates the game tree recursively to determine the optimal move by minimizing the possible losses for a worst-case scenario.

```python
# Define constants for players
PLAYER = 1   # AI
OPPONENT = -1  # Human Player

def evaluate(board):
    """
    Evaluate the board to determine if there's a winner.
    :param board: The current game board.
    :return: 1 if AI wins, -1 if human wins, 0 otherwise.
    """
    # Check rows for victory
    for row in board:
        if sum(row) == 3:
            return PLAYER
        if sum(row) == -3:
            return OPPONENT
    # Check columns for victory
    for col in range(len(board)):
        if board[0][col] + board[1][col] + board[2][col] == 3:
            return PLAYER
        if board[0][col] + board[1][col] + board[2][col] == -3:
            return OPPONENT
```

```python
    # Check diagonals for victory
    if board[0][0] + board[1][1] + board[2][2] == 3 or board[0][2] +
    ↪   board[1][1] + board[2][0] == 3:
        return PLAYER
    if board[0][0] + board[1][1] + board[2][2] == -3 or board[0][2]
    ↪   + board[1][1] + board[2][0] == -3:
        return OPPONENT
    return 0  # No winner yet

def is_moves_left(board):
    """
    Check if there are any moves left on the board.
    :param board: The current game board.
    :return: True if there are moves left, False otherwise.
    """
    for row in board:
        if 0 in row:
            return True
    return False

def minimax(board, depth, is_max):
    """
    Implementation of the minimax algorithm.
    :param board: The current game board.
    :param depth: Current depth in the game tree.
    :param is_max: Boolean indicating if the current move is
    ↪   maximizing.
    :return: The best score for the current board state.
    """
    score = evaluate(board)

    # If AI has won or lost the game, return the evaluation score
    if score == PLAYER:
        return score
    if score == OPPONENT:
        return score

    # If there are no moves left, it is a draw
    if not is_moves_left(board):
        return 0

    if is_max:
        best = -1000
        # Traverse the board to make the optimal move
        for i in range(3):
            for j in range(3):
                if board[i][j] == 0:  # Check empty spots
                    board[i][j] = PLAYER
                    best = max(best, minimax(board, depth + 1, not
                    ↪   is_max))
                    board[i][j] = 0  # Undo the move
        return best
    else:
```

```
            best = 1000
            # Traverse the board to make the optimal move
            for i in range(3):
                for j in range(3):
                    if board[i][j] == 0:   # Check empty spots
                        board[i][j] = OPPONENT
                        best = min(best, minimax(board, depth + 1, not
                        ↪  is_max))
                        board[i][j] = 0   # Undo the move
            return best

def find_best_move(board):
    """
    Determine the best move for the AI player.
    :param board: The current game board.
    :return: The best move coordinates.
    """
    best_val = -1000
    best_move = (-1, -1)
    for i in range(3):
        for j in range(3):
            if board[i][j] == 0:
                board[i][j] = PLAYER
                move_val = minimax(board, 0, False)
                board[i][j] = 0
                if move_val > best_val:
                    best_move = (i, j)
                    best_val = move_val
    return best_move

# Example usage: Finding the best move for the AI
current_board = [
    [1, -1, 0],
    [0, 1, 0],
    [-1, 0, 0]
]
best_move = find_best_move(current_board)
print("The best move for the AI is:", best_move)
```

This code defines the essential functions required for implementing the minimax algorithm in a game like Tic-Tac-Toe:

- evaluate function assesses the current board state to determine a winner.

- is_moves_left checks if any moves are still possible on the
  board.

- minimax represents the recursive core of the algorithm, exploring possible game states to find optimal strategies.

- **`find_best_move`** evaluates potential moves for the AI player and selects the most advantageous one.

The example at the end demonstrates finding the best move for the AI using a partially completed Tic-Tac-Toe board.

Chapter 63

Alpha-Beta Pruning Optimization

Below is a Python code snippet that showcases the implementation of the alpha-beta pruning algorithm to enhance the efficiency of the minimax strategy in game decision-making. This code includes methods for performing the minimax search, incorporating alpha-beta pruning, and an example call to demonstrate its application.

```
import math

def minimax(depth, node_index, maximizing_player, values, alpha,
↪   beta):
    '''
    Perform the minimax algorithm with alpha-beta pruning.
    :param depth: Current depth in the game tree.
    :param node_index: Index of the current node in the tree.
    :param maximizing_player: Boolean indicating if the current move
    ↪   is for the maximizing player.
    :param values: Terminal values at the leaves of the tree.
    :param alpha: Best score that the maximizer currently can
    ↪   guarantee at that level or above.
    :param beta: Best score that the minimizer currently can
    ↪   guarantee at that level or above.
    :return: Optimal value for the current player's move.
    '''
    # If we have reached the depth (leaf node), return the value of
    ↪   the node
    if depth == 3:
        return values[node_index]

    if maximizing_player:
```

```
        best = -math.inf
        # Recur for left and right children
        for i in range(0, 2):
            val = minimax(depth + 1, node_index * 2 + i, False,
            ↪ values, alpha, beta)
            best = max(best, val)
            alpha = max(alpha, best)
            # Alpha Beta Pruning
            if beta <= alpha:
                break
        return best
    else:
        best = math.inf
        # Recur for left and right children
        for i in range(0, 2):
            val = minimax(depth + 1, node_index * 2 + i, True,
            ↪ values, alpha, beta)
            best = min(best, val)
            beta = min(beta, best)
            # Alpha Beta Pruning
            if beta <= alpha:
                break
        return best

# Example tree: The terminal nodes in a game tree
values = [3, 5, 6, 9, 1, 2, 0, -1]

# Function call
optimal_value = minimax(0, 0, True, values, -math.inf, math.inf)
print("The optimal value is:", optimal_value)
```

This code defines the core components of the alpha-beta pruning implementation within the minimax algorithm:

- **minimax** function performs the actual search through the game tree leveraging alpha-beta pruning. It recursively evaluates the nodes of the game tree to determine the optimal move for maximizing or minimizing players.

- The algorithm uses **alpha** and **beta** to prune unnecessary branches in the search tree, thereby reducing the number of nodes evaluated, improving efficiency over the naive minimax approach.

- The example demonstrates computing the optimal move based on a simple pre-defined set of terminal node values, showcasing an optimal strategy's calculation within a bounded depth.

This illustrative example highlights how alpha-beta pruning optimizes decision-making efficiency in game-theoretical situations.

Chapter 64

Dijkstra's Algorithm in OSPF Routing

Below is a Python code snippet that implements Dijkstra's algorithm for computing the shortest paths in a graph. This implementation is tailored to showcase its application within the Open Shortest Path First (OSPF) routing protocol scenario and includes graph representation and route computation.

```python
import heapq

class Graph:
    def __init__(self):
        self.nodes = set()
        self.edges = {}
        self.distances = {}

    def add_node(self, value):
        self.nodes.add(value)
        self.edges[value] = []

    def add_edge(self, from_node, to_node, distance):
        self.edges[from_node].append(to_node)
        self.edges[to_node].append(from_node)  # Assuming undirected
        ↪ graph
        self.distances[(from_node, to_node)] = distance
        self.distances[(to_node, from_node)] = distance  # Assuming
        ↪ undirected graph

def dijkstra(graph, start_node):
    shortest_paths = {node: float('inf') for node in graph.nodes}
    shortest_paths[start_node] = 0
```

```
    priority_queue = [(0, start_node)]
    heapq.heapify(priority_queue)

    while priority_queue:
        (current_distance, current_node) =
        ↪  heapq.heappop(priority_queue)

        for neighbor in graph.edges[current_node]:
            distance = current_distance +
            ↪  graph.distances[(current_node, neighbor)]

            if distance < shortest_paths[neighbor]:
                shortest_paths[neighbor] = distance
                heapq.heappush(priority_queue, (distance, neighbor))

    return shortest_paths

# Example usage
g = Graph()
g.add_node("A")
g.add_node("B")
g.add_node("C")
g.add_node("D")

g.add_edge("A", "B", 1)
g.add_edge("A", "C", 3)
g.add_edge("B", "C", 1)
g.add_edge("B", "D", 2)
g.add_edge("C", "D", 5)

shortest_paths_from_A = dijkstra(g, "A")
print("Shortest paths from A:", shortest_paths_from_A)
```

This code defines a **Graph** class and a `dijkstra` function to perform the shortest path calculation:

- **Graph** class represents a simple graph structure with nodes and edges. It uses an adjacency list to manage graph connectivity and a dictionary to store edge distances.

- **add_node** method adds a node to the graph.

- **add_edge** method adds an undirected edge between two nodes with a specified distance.

- **dijkstra** function implements Dijkstra's algorithm to compute the shortest path from the start node to all other nodes in the graph, utilizing a priority queue for efficient extraction of the next node with the smallest tentative distance.

The example usage demonstrates creating a graph, adding nodes and edges, and then computing and printing the shortest paths from a specified node. This setup can be adapted to model scenarios in OSPF routing where route computation based on shortest paths is crucial.

Chapter 65

Spanning Tree Protocol (STP) in Network Design

Below is a Python code snippet that illustrates a basic implementation of the Spanning Tree Protocol (STP), which is used to create loop-free topologies in Ethernet networks. This example includes the computation of the spanning tree using a simplified version of the STP algorithm, using graph representations and redundancy elimination strategies.

```python
import networkx as nx

def spanning_tree_protocol(graph):
    '''
    Apply a simplified Spanning Tree Protocol to find a loop-free
    ↪ topology.
    :param graph: A NetworkX graph representing the network
    ↪ topology.
    :return: A graph representing the spanning tree.
    '''
    # Ensure the graph is connected
    if not nx.is_connected(graph):
        raise ValueError("Graph must be connected.")

    # Use NetworkX to find the minimum spanning tree
    mst = nx.minimum_spanning_tree(graph, algorithm='prim')

    return mst
```

```python
def add_bridge(graph, u, v, weight):
    '''
    Add an edge (bridge) to the network graph.
    :param graph: A NetworkX graph where the bridge will be added.
    :param u: The starting vertex of the bridge.
    :param v: The ending vertex of the bridge.
    :param weight: The weight of the bridge, representing the cost.
    '''
    graph.add_edge(u, v, weight=weight)

def create_network():
    '''
    Create a sample network topology using NetworkX.
    :return: A NetworkX graph representing the created network.
    '''
    G = nx.Graph()
    add_bridge(G, 'A', 'B', 1.0)
    add_bridge(G, 'A', 'C', 2.0)
    add_bridge(G, 'B', 'C', 1.0)
    add_bridge(G, 'B', 'D', 4.0)
    add_bridge(G, 'C', 'D', 1.0)
    add_bridge(G, 'C', 'E', 3.0)
    add_bridge(G, 'D', 'E', 2.0)
    return G

# Create the network topology
network = create_network()

# Compute the spanning tree
spanning_tree = spanning_tree_protocol(network)

# Display the Minimum Spanning Tree
print("Edges in the Spanning Tree:")
for edge in spanning_tree.edges(data=True):
    print(edge)

# Output: Edges in the Spanning Tree
# ('A', 'B', {'weight': 1.0})
# ('B', 'C', {'weight': 1.0})
# ('C', 'D', {'weight': 1.0})
# ('D', 'E', {'weight': 2.0})
```

This code defines several functions and demonstrates a simplified use of the Spanning Tree Protocol to ensure a loop-free topology within an Ethernet network:

- `spanning_tree_protocol` is a key function that computes the spanning tree for a given network graph, eliminating cycles and redundancies.

- `add_bridge` function is used to build the network by adding edges (bridges) between nodes with associated weights.

- `create_network` provides a sample network topology using the `add_bridge` function, which will then be processed to find a spanning tree.

- The script concludes by creating a network, processing it through the STP algorithm, and printing the edges that form the minimum spanning tree.

The code employs the NetworkX library to handle graph operations, ensuring efficient computation of the spanning tree.

Chapter 66

FP-Growth Algorithm for Frequent Pattern Mining

Below is a Python code snippet implementing the FP-Growth algorithm used for mining frequent itemsets. The code constructs an FP-tree and extracts frequent patterns without candidate generation.

```python
from collections import defaultdict, namedtuple
import itertools

class FPNode:
    def __init__(self, name, count, parent):
        self.name = name
        self.count = count
        self.parent = parent
        self.children = {}
        self.link = None

    def increment(self, count):
        self.count += count

class FPTree:
    def __init__(self, transactions, min_support):
        self.root = FPNode(None, 1, None)
        self.min_support = min_support
        self.header_table = defaultdict(list)
        self.frequent_itemsets = []
        self.build_tree(transactions)
```

```python
def build_tree(self, transactions):
    item_count = defaultdict(int)
    for transaction in transactions:
        for item in transaction:
            item_count[item] += 1

    item_count = {item: count for item, count in
    ↪   item_count.items() if count >= self.min_support}
    if not item_count:
        return

    for item, count in sorted(item_count.items(), key=lambda x:
    ↪   (-x[1], x[0])):
        self.header_table[item] = [None, count]

    for transaction in transactions:
        filtered_items = sorted([item for item in transaction if
        ↪   item in item_count],
                                key=lambda item:
                                ↪   (-item_count[item], item))
        self._insert_tree(filtered_items, self.root)

def _insert_tree(self, items, node):
    if not items:
        return
    first_item = items[0]
    if first_item in node.children:
        node.children[first_item].increment(1)
    else:
        new_node = FPNode(first_item, 1, node)
        node.children[first_item] = new_node
        if self.header_table[first_item][0] is None:
            self.header_table[first_item][0] = new_node
        else:
            current_node = self.header_table[first_item][0]
            while current_node.link is not None:
                current_node = current_node.link
            current_node.link = new_node

    self._insert_tree(items[1:], node.children[first_item])

def find_frequent_itemsets(self):
    for item in self.header_table:
        self._find_frequent_patterns(item, [],
        ↪   self.header_table.copy())
    return self.frequent_itemsets

def _find_frequent_patterns(self, item, suffix, header):
    nodes = []
    linkage_node = header[item][0]
    while linkage_node is not None:
        parent_nodes = []
        parent = linkage_node.parent
```

```
            while parent.name is not None:
                parent_nodes.append(parent.name)
                parent = parent.parent
            for _ in range(linkage_node.count):
                nodes.append(parent_nodes)
            linkage_node = linkage_node.link

        subtree = FPTree(nodes, self.min_support)
        for subtree_item in header[item:]:
            subtree.header_table[subtree_item][0] = None
        subtree.build_tree(nodes)
        subtree_patterns = subtree.find_frequent_itemsets()

        for pattern in subtree_patterns:
            self.frequent_itemsets.append(pattern + [item])

# Sample use case
transactions = [['milk', 'bread', 'butter'],
                ['beer', 'bread'],
                ['milk', 'beer', 'bread', 'butter'],
                ['beer', 'butter']]
min_support = 2
fp_tree = FPTree(transactions, min_support)
frequent_itemsets = fp_tree.find_frequent_itemsets()

print(f"Frequent itemsets: {frequent_itemsets}")
```

This code defines the essential structures and functions for implementing the FP-Growth algorithm:

- **FPNode** class represents a node in the FP-tree and tracks item occurrences.

- **FPTree** class builds the tree based on transactional data and minimum support threshold.

- **_insert_tree** method inserts items into the FP-tree recursively.

- **find_frequent_itemsets** method extracts all itemsets meeting the minimum support by navigating the header table.

- **_find_frequent_patterns** recursively finds frequent patterns for each item in the header table.

The sample use case demonstrates constructing an FP-tree from a list of transactions and finding frequent itemsets based on the given minimum support.

Chapter 67

Push-Relabel Algorithm for Maximum Flow

Below is a Python code snippet that provides a detailed implementation of the push-relabel algorithm for computing maximum flow in a network, along with the necessary functions for label management and discharge operations.

```python
from collections import defaultdict, deque

class PushRelabel:
    def __init__(self, vertex_count):
        self.vertex_count = vertex_count
        self.flow = defaultdict(lambda: defaultdict(int))
        self.capacity = defaultdict(lambda: defaultdict(int))
        self.height = [0] * vertex_count
        self.excess = [0] * vertex_count

    def add_edge(self, u, v, capacity):
        ''' Add edge to the flow network and record its capacity.
        ↪    '''
        self.capacity[u][v] = capacity

    def push(self, u, v):
        ''' Push flow from vertex u to vertex v. '''
        send = min(self.excess[u], self.capacity[u][v] -
        ↪    self.flow[u][v])
        self.flow[u][v] += send
        self.flow[v][u] -= send
        self.excess[u] -= send
```

```
                self.excess[v] += send

    def relabel(self, u):
        ''' Relabel vertex u to find a viable height to push flow.
        ↪     '''
        min_height = float('inf')
        for v in self.capacity[u]:
            if self.capacity[u][v] - self.flow[u][v] > 0:
                min_height = min(min_height, self.height[v])
        if min_height < float('inf'):
            self.height[u] = min_height + 1

    def discharge(self, u):
        ''' Discharge excess flow from vertex u to its neighbors.
        ↪     '''
        while self.excess[u] > 0:
            for v in self.capacity[u]:
                if self.capacity[u][v] - self.flow[u][v] > 0 and
                ↪     self.height[u] > self.height[v]:
                    self.push(u, v)
                    if self.excess[u] == 0:
                        break
            else:
                self.relabel(u)

    def max_flow(self, source, sink):
        ''' Compute maximum flow from source to sink. '''
        self.height[source] = self.vertex_count
        self.excess[source] = float('inf')
        for v in self.capacity[source]:
            self.push(source, v)

        active_vertices = deque(u for u in range(self.vertex_count)
        ↪     if u != source and u != sink and self.excess[u] > 0)

        while active_vertices:
            u = active_vertices.popleft()
            old_height = self.height[u]
            self.discharge(u)
            if self.height[u] > old_height:
                active_vertices.appendleft(u)

        return sum(self.flow[source][v] for v in
        ↪     self.capacity[source])

# Example usage
vertex_count = 6
network = PushRelabel(vertex_count)
edges = [
    (0, 1, 16), (0, 2, 13), (1, 2, 10), (1, 3, 12),
    (2, 1, 4), (2, 4, 14), (3, 2, 9), (3, 5, 20),
    (4, 3, 7), (4, 5, 4)
]
```

209

```
for u, v, cap in edges:
    network.add_edge(u, v, cap)

source, sink = 0, 5
max_flow_value = network.max_flow(source, sink)
print(f"The maximum flow from vertex {source} to vertex {sink} is
↪ {max_flow_value}")
```

This code defines the essential functions for implementing the push-relabel algorithm for maximum flow in networks:

- **add_edge** method establishes directed edges in the network with specified capacities.

- **push** function executes the push operation of flow between adjacent vertices, updating excess and flow amounts.

- **relabel** recalibrates the height of a vertex to maintain feasibility of the preflow.

- **discharge** method actively pushes excess flow from a vertex until its excess is zero or relabeling is needed.

- **max_flow** integrates all operations to determine the maximum flow from source to sink.

The example provided computes the maximum flow in a small network, demonstrating the intended usage of the algorithm.

Chapter 68

Edmonds' Algorithm for Optimum Branchings

Below is a Python code snippet that demonstrates the implementation of Edmonds' algorithm, also known as the Chu-Liu/Edmonds' algorithm, for finding an optimal spanning tree in a directed graph with applications in network design and ranking.

```python
class Graph:
    def __init__(self, vertices):
        self.V = vertices
        self.adj = [[] for _ in range(vertices)]

    def add_edge(self, u, v, weight):
        self.adj[u].append((v, weight))

def edmonds(graph, root):
    import heapq

    def min_incoming_edge(graph, root):
        # Initialize distances with infinity
        dist = [float('inf')] * graph.V
        # Each vertex reaches itself with cost 0
        dist[root] = 0
        # For each vertex, find the minimum incoming edge
        for u in range(graph.V):
            for v, weight in graph.adj[u]:
                if weight < dist[v]:
                    dist[v] = weight
                    parent[v] = u
```

```python
def cycle_detection(parent):
    visited = [-1] * graph.V
    cycle_nodes = []
    # Start DFS from the root
    for i in range(graph.V):
        if visited[i] == -1:  # If not visited
            u = i
            while u != -1 and visited[u] == -1:
                visited[u] = i  # Mark the node with the start
                ↪    index
                u = parent[u]
            if u != -1 and visited[u] == i:
                v = u
                cycle_nodes.append(u)
                # Trace the cycle
                u = parent[u]
                while u != v:
                    cycle_nodes.append(u)
                    u = parent[u]
    return cycle_nodes

def contract_cycle(graph, cycle_nodes):
    contracted = set(cycle_nodes)
    new_graph = Graph(graph.V)
    for u in range(graph.V):
        if u not in contracted:
            new_graph.adj[u] = [(v, w) for v, w in graph.adj[u]
            ↪    if v not in contracted]
            for node in cycle_nodes:
                for v, weight in graph.adj[node]:
                    if v not in contracted:
                        new_graph.adj[u].append((v, weight))
                        break
    return new_graph

# Initialize parent and mst_cost
parent = [-1] * graph.V
mst_cost = 0

# Run the minimum incoming edge subroutine
min_incoming_edge(graph, root)

# Detect cycles
cycle_nodes = cycle_detection(parent)
if not cycle_nodes:
    # No cycle detected, calculate total cost
    mst_cost += sum(dist)
else:
    # Contract cycle and recursively call Edmonds' algorithm
    contracted_graph = contract_cycle(graph, cycle_nodes)
    mst_cost += edmonds(contracted_graph, root)
```

```
    return mst_cost

# Example usage
graph = Graph(5)
graph.add_edge(0, 1, 2)
graph.add_edge(1, 2, 3)
graph.add_edge(2, 3, 1)
graph.add_edge(3, 4, 4)
graph.add_edge(4, 0, 5)
root = 0
mst_cost = edmonds(graph, root)
print("Minimum Spanning Tree Cost:", mst_cost)
```

This code defines several key components necessary for implementing Edmonds' algorithm to find an optimal spanning tree in
a directed graph:

- **Graph** class represents a directed graph, storing vertices and
  edges.

- **add_edge** method adds a directed edge from vertex u to vertex v with a specified weight.

- **edmonds** function implements the core of the algorithm, including steps for detecting cycles, computing minimum incoming edges, and handling contractions.

- **min_incoming_edge** function processes incoming edges at each
  vertex to identify minimum cost edges.

- **cycle_detection** function checks for cycles in the graph and
  returns the set of nodes forming a cycle.

- **contract_cycle** function rebuilds the graph structure post-
  cycle detection for recursive processing.

The example at the end demonstrates the creation of a graph
and calculation of the minimum spanning tree cost using Edmonds'
algorithm.

Chapter 69

Bellman-Ford-Moore Algorithm for Shortest Paths

Below is a Python code snippet implementing the Bellman-Ford-Moore algorithm for computing shortest paths in graphs with potential negative weight edges and detecting negative cycles.

```python
class Graph:
    def __init__(self, vertices):
        self.V = vertices      # Number of vertices
        self.edges = []        # List to store graph edges

    def add_edge(self, u, v, w):
        '''Add an edge to the graph'''
        self.edges.append((u, v, w))

    def bellman_ford(self, src):
        '''Run Bellman-Ford algorithm from a source vertex and
        ↪   detect negative cycles'''
        # Initialize distances from src to all other vertices as
        ↪   infinite
        dist = [float("Inf")] * self.V
        dist[src] = 0

        # Relaxation of all edges 'V-1' times
        for _ in range(self.V - 1):
            for u, v, w in self.edges:
                if dist[u] != float("Inf") and dist[u] + w <
                ↪   dist[v]:
                    dist[v] = dist[u] + w
```

```
        # Check for negative-weight cycles
        for u, v, w in self.edges:
            if dist[u] != float("Inf") and dist[u] + w < dist[v]:
                print("Graph contains a negative weight cycle")
                return None

        # Return the shortest distance array
        return dist

if __name__ == '__main__':
    # Create a graph with 5 vertices
    graph = Graph(5)
    graph.add_edge(0, 1, -1)
    graph.add_edge(0, 2, 4)
    graph.add_edge(1, 2, 3)
    graph.add_edge(1, 3, 2)
    graph.add_edge(1, 4, 2)
    graph.add_edge(3, 2, 5)
    graph.add_edge(3, 1, 1)
    graph.add_edge(4, 3, -3)

    # Compute shortest paths from vertex 0
    distances = graph.bellman_ford(0)

    # Print computed shortest distances
    if distances:
        for i, d in enumerate(distances):
            print(f"Distance from vertex 0 to vertex {i} is {d}")
```

This code defines a class-based approach to represent a graph and implements the **bellman_ford** method as follows:

- **Graph** class stores the number of vertices and edges of the graph.

- **add_edge** method allows for adding edges with weights to the graph.

- **bellman_ford** method runs the Bellman-Ford algorithm for a given source vertex, relaxing edges to compute shortest paths and checking for negative weight cycles.

- If a negative weight cycle is detected, the code outputs a warning and returns **None**.

- The final block of the code demonstrates how to create a graph, add edges, compute shortest paths, and output the shortest distance from the source vertex.

Chapter 70

Four Russians Algorithm for Boolean Matrix Multiplication

Below is a Python code snippet that demonstrates the implementation of the Four Russians technique applied to boolean matrix multiplication and transitive closure computations.

```python
import numpy as np

def bit_combinations(bits):
    return [bin(i)[2:].zfill(bits) for i in range(1 << bits)]

def preprocess_boothrussians(A, B):
    '''
    Preprocess step of the Four Russians method for boolean matrix
    ↪ multiplication.
    :param A: Boolean matrix A (m x q).
    :param B: Boolean matrix B (q x n).
    :return: Preprocessed lookup table.
    '''
    m, q = A.shape
    q, n = B.shape
    s = np.ceil(np.log2(q)).astype(int)  # Block size
    P = dict()

    for comb in bit_combinations(s):
        binary_vector = np.array(list(map(int, comb[::-1])))
        P[comb] = A[:, :s] @ binary_vector

    return P
```

```python
def four_russians_multiplication(A, B):
    '''
    Apply the Four Russians method to multiply boolean matrices A
    ↪   and B.
    :param A: Boolean matrix A (m x q).
    :param B: Boolean matrix B (q x n).
    :return: Boolean matrix C (m x n), result of A * B.
    '''
    m, q = A.shape
    q, n = B.shape
    C = np.zeros((m, n), dtype=bool)
    P = preprocess_boothrussians(A, B)

    s = np.ceil(np.log2(q)).astype(int)

    for step in range((q + s - 1) // s):
        part_B = B[step * s:(step + 1) * s, :]
        B_combined = np.sum((2**np.arange(part_B.shape[0]))[:, None]
        ↪   * part_B, axis=0)

        for i in range(n):
            C[:, i] += P[bin(B_combined[i])[2:].zfill(s)]

    return C.astype(bool)

def boolean_transitive_closure(adj_matrix):
    '''
    Compute the transitive closure of a boolean adjacency matrix
    ↪   using Four Russians.
    :param adj_matrix: Boolean adjacency matrix (n x n).
    :return: Boolean matrix representing transitive closure.
    '''
    n, _ = adj_matrix.shape
    closure = adj_matrix.copy()
    prev_closure = np.zeros_like(closure)

    while not np.array_equal(closure, prev_closure):
        prev_closure = closure.copy()
        closure = four_russians_multiplication(closure, adj_matrix)
        ↪   | closure

    return closure

# Example usage
if __name__ == "__main__":
    A = np.array([[1, 1, 0], [0, 1, 1], [1, 0, 1]], dtype=bool)
    B = np.array([[1, 0, 1], [1, 1, 0], [0, 1, 1]], dtype=bool)

    C = four_russians_multiplication(A, B)
    print("Result of Boolean Matrix Multiplication C:")
    print(C)
```

```
adj_matrix = np.array([[1, 1, 0], [0, 1, 1], [1, 0, 1]],
↪  dtype=bool)
transitive_closure_result =
↪  boolean_transitive_closure(adj_matrix)
print("Result of Transitive Closure:")
print(transitive_closure_result)
```

This code provides a detailed implementation of the Four Russians technique through the following key functions:

- `bit_combinations` generates all possible combinations of binary vectors of a given length.

- `preprocess_boothrussians` sets up a lookup table by preprocessing partial results for fast retrieval during multiplication.

- `four_russians_multiplication` performs boolean matrix multiplication using the Four Russians technique, leveraging the preprocessed table for efficiency.

- `boolean_transitive_closure` computes the transitive closure of a boolean matrix to identify reachability across nodes using repeated application of the multiplication function.

The example usage showcases the application of these functions to boolean matrices, demonstrating their calculations and outputs.

Chapter 71

Prediction by Partial Matching (PPM) Compression

Below is a Python code snippet that demonstrates the implementation of Prediction by Partial Matching (PPM) used in data compression, focusing on order-k models and escape mechanisms to effectively predict and encode data sequences.

```python
class PPM:
    def __init__(self, order):
        self.order = order
        self.context = {}

    def update_context(self, seq):
        '''
        Update the context model with the given sequence.
        :param seq: Sequence of characters to update context with.
        '''
        for i in range(len(seq)):
            for j in range(1, self.order + 1):
                if i + j <= len(seq):
                    context = tuple(seq[i:i + j - 1])
                    symbol = seq[i + j - 1]
                    if context not in self.context:
                        self.context[context] = {}
                    if symbol not in self.context[context]:
                        self.context[context][symbol] = 0
                    self.context[context][symbol] += 1

    def get_total_frequency(self, context):
```

```
    ' ' '
    Get the total frequency of all symbols in the given context.
    :param context: Context to calculate total frequency for.
    :return: Total frequency of symbols in the context.
    ' ' '
    return sum(self.context.get(context, {}).values())

def escape_mechanism(self, context):
    ' ' '
    Handle unknown symbols with escape mechanism in the context.
    :param context: Context to determine escape handling.
    :return: Escape frequency.
    ' ' '
    return len(self.context.get(context, {})) or 1

def predict(self, seq):
    ' ' '
    Predict the next symbol based on the given sequence.
    :param seq: Sequence of characters for prediction.
    :return: Dictionary of symbol probabilities.
    ' ' '
    prediction = {}
    for j in range(self.order, 0, -1):
        context = tuple(seq[-j:])
        if context in self.context:
            total_freq = self.get_total_frequency(context)
            escape_freq = self.escape_mechanism(context)
            for symbol, freq in self.context[context].items():
                prediction[symbol] = freq / (total_freq +
                ↪    escape_freq)
            prediction['_ESCAPE'] = escape_freq / (total_freq +
            ↪    escape_freq)
            break
    return prediction or {'default': 1.0}

def encode_sequence(self, seq):
    ' ' '
    Encode a sequence using the PPM model.
    :param seq: Sequence of characters to encode.
    :return: List of encoded values.
    ' ' '
    encoded_seq = []
    self.update_context(seq)
    for i in range(len(seq)):
        context = tuple(seq[max(0, i-self.order):i])
        prediction = self.predict(context)
        symbol = seq[i]
        if symbol not in prediction:
            encoded_seq.append(prediction.get('_ESCAPE', 0))
        encoded_seq.append(prediction.get(symbol, 0))
    return encoded_seq

# Example usage
```

```
ppm_model = PPM(order=3)
sequence = "abracadabra"
ppm_model.update_context(sequence)
encoded_sequence = ppm_model.encode_sequence(sequence)

print("Encoded Sequence:", encoded_sequence)
```

This code provides a straightforward implementation of the **Prediction by Partial Matching (PPM)** compression technique:

- **PPM** class encapsulates the data model for a given order.

- **update_context** method updates the model with sequences by adjusting frequencies of symbols in various contexts.

- **get_total_frequency** calculates the sum of frequencies for all symbols within a given context.

- **escape_mechanism** provides an escape strategy for scenarios where a symbol doesn't match known contexts.

- **predict** generates probabilities for possible next symbols or an escape option in case of novel sequences.

- **encode_sequence** method serializes a sequence into encoded representation based on context-derived predictions.

The provided example showcases usage of the PPM model with a simple character sequence highlighting the core operations of context management, escape handling, and sequence encoding.

Chapter 72

Context Mixing Algorithms for Data Compression

Below is a Python code snippet that demonstrates the core components of a context mixing algorithm used in the PAQ series for data compression. The implementation focuses on model initialization, prediction, and update mechanisms, leveraging multiple models to enhance predictive accuracy.

```python
import numpy as np

class ContextModel:
    def __init__(self, contexts=256):
        '''
        Initialize context model with given size.
        :param contexts: Number of different contexts to track.
        '''
        self.contexts = contexts
        self.probability_tables = np.ones((contexts, 2)) / 2  #
        ↪  start with neutral probabilities

    def predict(self, context):
        '''
        Predict next symbol probability distribution.
        :param context: Current context index.
        :return: Probability of symbol being 1.
        '''
        return self.probability_tables[context, 1]
```

```python
    def update(self, context, symbol):
        '''
        Update probability tables based on new symbol.
        :param context: Current context index.
        :param symbol: Actual observed symbol (0 or 1).
        '''
        self.probability_tables[context, symbol] += 0.1
        # Normalization
        total = sum(self.probability_tables[context])
        self.probability_tables[context] /= total

def model_prediction(symbols, context_fn):
    '''
    Simulate prediction using multiple context models.
    :param symbols: Sequence of observed symbols.
    :param context_fn: Function to extract context from symbol
    ↪   sequence.
    :return: List of predictions for each symbol.
    '''
    model = ContextModel()
    predictions = []
    for i in range(1, len(symbols)):
        context = context_fn(symbols[:i])
        prediction = model.predict(context)
        predictions.append(prediction)
        model.update(context, symbols[i])
    return predictions

def binary_context(symbol_sequence):
    '''
    Example context function generating binary context.
    :param symbol_sequence: Current sequence of symbols.
    :return: Context index for current sequence.
    '''
    return int(''.join(map(str, symbol_sequence[-3:])), 2) if
    ↪   len(symbol_sequence) >= 3 else 0

# Example usage with a simple binary sequence
sequence = [0, 1, 1, 0, 1, 0, 1, 1, 0, 0, 1]
predictions = model_prediction(sequence, binary_context)

print("Predictions:", predictions)
```

This code provides the foundational elements of a context mixing implementation in data compression:

- `ContextModel` class manages probabilities associated with different contexts, initially set to neutral.

- `predict` method outputs the probability of the next symbol being 1, based on the current context.

223

- **update** method adjusts the probability estimates after observing each new symbol.

- **model_prediction** function simulates compressive prediction across a symbol sequence, utilizing context-driven model predictions and updates.

- **binary_context** provides an example of extracting context indices from the most recent three symbols in the sequence.

The example demonstrates how this algorithm predicts subsequent symbols in a binary sequence using basic context information.

Chapter 73

Branch and Bound Algorithms for Optimization

Below is a Python code snippet that encompasses the core computational elements of branch and bound techniques including the problem definition, bounding and pruning functions, and strategies for traversing the search tree to find an optimal solution.

```python
import sys
import numpy as np

def branch_and_bound_knapsack(weights, profits, capacity):
    '''
    Solve the knapsack problem using the Branch and Bound method.
    :param weights: List of weights for each item.
    :param profits: List of profits for each item.
    :param capacity: Maximum capacity of the knapsack.
    :return: Maximum profit and the list of items included in the
    ↪  optimal solution.
    '''

    class Node:
        def __init__(self, level, profit, weight, bound, items):
            self.level = level
            self.profit = profit
            self.weight = weight
            self.bound = bound
            self.items = items

    def bound(node, n, W, profits, weights):
```

```
'''
Calculate the upper bound on maximum profit in the subtree
↪   rooted at node.
:param node: The current node being evaluated.
:param n: Total number of items.
:param W: Maximum capacity of the knapsack.
:param profits: List of profits for each item.
:param weights: List of weights for each item.
:return: Bound value.
'''
if node.weight >= W:
    return 0

profit_bound = node.profit
j = node.level + 1
totweight = node.weight

# Check index range and calculate bound
while j < n and totweight + weights[j] <= W:
    totweight += weights[j]
    profit_bound += profits[j]
    j += 1

# If j is not the last item, use fraction of the weight left
if j < n:
    profit_bound += (W - totweight) * profits[j] /
    ↪   weights[j]

return profit_bound

# Sort items based on profit/weight ratio
n = len(weights)
items = list(range(n))
items.sort(key=lambda i: profits[i] / weights[i], reverse=True)
weights = [weights[i] for i in items]
profits = [profits[i] for i in items]

queue = []
root = Node(-1, 0, 0, 0.0, [])
root.bound = bound(root, n, capacity, profits, weights)
max_profit = 0
best_items = []

queue.append(root)
while queue:
    current_node = queue.pop(0)

    if current_node.level == -1:
        next_level = 0
    else:
        next_level = current_node.level + 1

    if next_level < n:
```

226

```
            left_node = Node(next_level,
                             current_node.profit +
                             ↪ profits[next_level],
                             current_node.weight +
                             ↪ weights[next_level],
                             0.0,
                             current_node.items +
                             ↪ [items[next_level]])
            left_node.bound = bound(left_node, n, capacity, profits,
            ↪ weights)

            if left_node.weight <= capacity and left_node.profit >
            ↪ max_profit:
                max_profit = left_node.profit
                best_items = left_node.items

            if left_node.bound > max_profit:
                queue.append(left_node)

            right_node = Node(next_level,
                              current_node.profit,
                              current_node.weight,
                              0.0,
                              current_node.items)
            right_node.bound = bound(right_node, n, capacity,
            ↪ profits, weights)

            if right_node.bound > max_profit:
                queue.append(right_node)

    return max_profit, best_items

# Example use case with weights, profits, and capacity
weights = [2, 3, 4, 5]
profits = [3, 4, 5, 6]
capacity = 5
max_profit, items_included = branch_and_bound_knapsack(weights,
↪ profits, capacity)

print("Maximum Profit:", max_profit)
print("Items Included:", items_included)
```

This code defines several key functions necessary for the implementation of branch and bound techniques for the knapsack problem:

- `branch_and_bound_knapsack` function uses nodes to explore different combinations of items that can be included in the knapsack and uses bounds to prune non-promising branches.

- `Node` class describes the level of a decision tree, the current profit, the current weight, the bound for the node, and the list of items included.

- **bound** function calculates an upper bound on the possible profit from a given node, enabling the algorithm to prune branches that cannot contain an optimal solution.

The output of the code will give the maximum profit that can be packed in the knapsack and the items included in that optimal solution.

Chapter 74

Simulated Annealing for Global Optimization

Below is a Python code snippet that encompasses the core computational elements of simulated annealing, including the implementation of temperature schedules, energy function evaluation, and handling the escape from local optima during the optimization process.

```python
import numpy as np
import random

def simulated_annealing(initial_state, energy_function,
↪    neighbor_function, temperature_function, max_iterations):
    '''
    Perform simulated annealing to find the state with the minimum
    ↪    energy.
    :param initial_state: Starting state for the algorithm.
    :param energy_function: Function to calculate energy for a given
    ↪    state.
    :param neighbor_function: Function to generate a neighboring
    ↪    state.
    :param temperature_function: Function to calculate temperature
    ↪    at iteration.
    :param max_iterations: Maximum number of iterations to run the
    ↪    algorithm.
    :return: Best state encountered and its energy.
    '''

    current_state = initial_state
```

```python
    current_energy = energy_function(current_state)
    best_state = current_state
    best_energy = current_energy

    for iteration in range(max_iterations):
        temperature = temperature_function(iteration)
        if temperature == 0:
            break

        neighbor = neighbor_function(current_state)
        neighbor_energy = energy_function(neighbor)

        if neighbor_energy < current_energy or random.random() <
        ↪   np.exp((current_energy - neighbor_energy) /
        ↪   temperature):
            current_state = neighbor
            current_energy = neighbor_energy

            if current_energy < best_energy:
                best_state = current_state
                best_energy = current_energy

    return best_state, best_energy

# Example of usage:

def energy_function_example(state):
    # An example energy function: finding the minimum of a quadratic
    ↪   function
    return state ** 2

def neighbor_function_example(state):
    # Small random step around the current state
    return state + random.uniform(-1, 1)

def temperature_function_example(iteration):
    # Example cooling schedule: Linear reduction
    return max(0.1, min(1.0, 1.0 - iteration / 1000))

initial_state_example = 10
max_iterations_example = 10000

best_state, best_energy = simulated_annealing(
    initial_state_example,
    energy_function_example,
    neighbor_function_example,
    temperature_function_example,
    max_iterations_example
)

print("Best state found:", best_state)
print("Energy of best state:", best_energy)
```

This code defines the essential components required for the implementation of simulated annealing:

- **simulated_annealing** is the main function performing the optimization process, adjusting current states based on the energy function and temperature schedule.

- **energy_function_example** serves as an illustrative energy function for calculating the "cost" of a given state.

- **neighbor_function_example** generates a nearby state, allowing the algorithm to explore the solution space.

- **temperature_function_example** demonstrates a simple cooling schedule that decreases linearly over iterations.

The final block of code provides an example usage of the simulated annealing algorithm to determine the minimum of a quadratic function.

Chapter 75

Genetic Algorithms in Search and Optimization

Below is a Python code snippet that implements a basic Genetic Algorithm, encapsulating essential operations such as selection, crossover, mutation, and fitness evaluation, which are fundamental to evolutionary computation.

```python
import random

def individual(length, min_value, max_value):
    '''
    Create a member of the population.
    :param length: Number of genes in the individual.
    :param min_value: Minimum value of a gene.
    :param max_value: Maximum value of a gene.
    :return: An individual as a list of genes.
    '''
    return [random.randint(min_value, max_value) for _ in
    ↪   range(length)]

def population(count, length, min_value, max_value):
    '''
    Create a population of individuals.
    :param count: Number of individuals in the population.
    :param length: Number of genes in an individual.
    :param min_value: Minimum value of a gene.
    :param max_value: Maximum value of a gene.
    :return: Population as a list of individuals.
    '''
```

```python
    return [individual(length, min_value, max_value) for _ in
    ↪  range(count)]

def fitness(individual, target):
    '''
    Determine the fitness of an individual.
    :param individual: The individual to evaluate.
    :param target: The target value for fitness evaluation.
    :return: The fitness value as an integer.
    '''
    return abs(target - sum(individual))

def grade(population, target):
    '''
    Calculate the average fitness of a population.
    :param population: The population to evaluate.
    :param target: The target value for fitness evaluation.
    :return: The average fitness.
    '''
    return sum(fitness(individual, target) for individual in
    ↪  population) / len(population)

def selection(population, target, retain=0.2):
    '''
    Select individuals for mating.
    :param population: The current population.
    :param target: The target value for fitness evaluation.
    :param retain: Proportion of population to retain.
    :return: List of selected individuals.
    '''
    graded = [(fitness(individual, target), individual) for
    ↪  individual in population]
    graded = [x[1] for x in sorted(graded)]
    retain_length = int(len(graded) * retain)
    return graded[:retain_length]

def crossover(parent1, parent2):
    '''
    Perform crossover between two parents to produce offspring.
    :param parent1: First parent individual.
    :param parent2: Second parent individual.
    :return: Two offspring individuals.
    '''
    if len(parent1) != len(parent2):
        raise ValueError("Parents must have the same length.")

    cut = random.randint(1, len(parent1) - 1)
    child1 = parent1[:cut] + parent2[cut:]
    child2 = parent2[:cut] + parent1[cut:]
    return child1, child2

def mutate(individual, min_value, max_value):
    '''
```

```
    Mutate an individual.
    :param individual: The individual to mutate.
    :param min_value: Minimum value of a gene.
    :param max_value: Maximum value of a gene.
    :return: Mutated individual.
    '''
    index = random.randrange(len(individual))
    individual[index] = random.randint(min_value, max_value)
    return individual

def evolve(population, target, min_value, max_value, eliminate=0.2,
↪  mutate_chance=0.1):
    '''
    Evolve a population through selection, crossover, and mutation.
    :param population: The current population.
    :param target: The target value for fitness evaluation.
    :param min_value: Minimum value of a gene.
    :param max_value: Maximum value of a gene.
    :param eliminate: Proportion of population to eliminate.
    :param mutate_chance: Chance of mutation for an individual.
    :return: Evolved population.
    '''
    selected = selection(population, target)
    offspring = []

    while len(offspring) < len(population):
        parent1, parent2 = random.sample(selected, 2)
        child1, child2 = crossover(parent1, parent2)

        if random.random() < mutate_chance:
            child1 = mutate(child1, min_value, max_value)
        if random.random() < mutate_chance:
            child2 = mutate(child2, min_value, max_value)

        offspring.extend([child1, child2])

    non_elites = int(len(offspring) * (1 - eliminate))
    return selected + offspring[:non_elites]

# Parameters
target = 100
population_count = 20
individual_length = 5
gene_min_value = 0
gene_max_value = 10

# Initial population
pop = population(population_count, individual_length,
↪  gene_min_value, gene_max_value)
fitness_history = [grade(pop, target)]

# Evolution steps
for _ in range(100):
```

```
pop = evolve(pop, target, gene_min_value, gene_max_value)
fitness_history.append(grade(pop, target))

print("Initial population's average fitness:", fitness_history[0])
print("Final population's average fitness:", fitness_history[-1])
```

This code demonstrates the essential components of a genetic algorithm:

- **individual** creates a single member of the population, with genes initialized between specified minimum and maximum values.

- **population** generates an initial population of individuals.

- **fitness** evaluates an individual's fitness based on the proximity to a target sum of its genes.

- **grade** computes the average fitness of the population.

- **selection** retains a portion of the best-performing individuals.

- **crossover** combines two parents to produce offspring with mixed genetic traits.

- **mutate** introduces random alterations to an individual's genes, maintaining genetic diversity.

- **evolve** iterates over the population, applying selection, crossover, and mutation to produce a new generation.

The example provided evolves a population towards a target sum, demonstrating the adaptive capabilities of genetic algorithms.

Chapter 76

Ukkonen's Algorithm for Online Suffix Tree Construction

Below is a Python code snippet that demonstrates the construction of a suffix tree using Ukkonen's algorithm, incorporating implicit suffix trees and optimization techniques.

```python
class Node:
    def __init__(self, start, end, suffix_link=None):
        self.start = start
        self.end = end
        self.suffix_link = suffix_link
        self.children = {}

class SuffixTree:
    def __init__(self, text):
        self.text = text
        self.root = Node(None, None)
        self.build()

    def build(self):
        n = len(self.text)
        self.root.suffix_link = self.root
        active_node = self.root
        active_edge = 0
        active_length = 0
        remainder = 0
        buffer_end = -1

        for i in range(n):
```

```python
buffer_end += 1
remainder += 1
last_new_node = None

while remainder > 0:
    if active_length == 0:
        active_edge = i

    if self.text[active_edge] not in
    ↪   active_node.children:
        leaf_node = Node(i, buffer_end)
        active_node.children[self.text[active_edge]] =
        ↪   leaf_node

        if last_new_node is not None:
            last_new_node.suffix_link = active_node
            last_new_node = None
    else:
        next =
        ↪   active_node.children[self.text[active_edge]]
        edge_length = next.end - next.start + 1
        if active_length >= edge_length:
            active_edge += edge_length
            active_length -= edge_length
            active_node = next
            continue

        if self.text[next.start + active_length] ==
        ↪   self.text[i]:
            if last_new_node is not None and active_node
            ↪   != self.root:
                last_new_node.suffix_link = active_node
                last_new_node = None

            active_length += 1
            break

        split_end = next.start + active_length - 1
        split_node = Node(next.start, split_end)
        active_node.children[self.text[active_edge]] =
        ↪   split_node

        leaf_node = Node(i, buffer_end)
        split_node.children[self.text[i]] = leaf_node
        next.start += active_length
        split_node.children[self.text[next.start]] =
        ↪   next

        if last_new_node is not None:
            last_new_node.suffix_link = split_node

        last_new_node = split_node
```

237

```
                    remainder -= 1

                    if active_node == self.root and active_length > 0:
                        active_length -= 1
                        active_edge = i - remainder + 1
                    else:
                        active_node = active_node.suffix_link if
                      ↪ active_node.suffix_link else self.root

def print_suffix_tree(node, text, depth=0):
    for k, c in node.children.items():
        edge = text[c.start:c.end+1]
        print(' ' * depth + f"{k}: {edge}")
        print_suffix_tree(c, text, depth + 2)

# Example usage
text = "xabxac#"
st = SuffixTree(text)
print_suffix_tree(st.root, text)
```

This code defines the core classes and functions for constructing a suffix tree using Ukkonen's algorithm:

- The `Node` class represents nodes in the suffix tree, storing start and end indices, suffix links, and children nodes.

- The `SuffixTree` class initializes with the given text and builds the suffix tree using Ukkonen's efficient method.

- The `build` function implements Ukkonen's algorithm, managing active points, remainder, and node splits to construct the tree.

- `print_suffix_tree` is a utility function to print the suffix tree structure for visualization purposes.

An example usage demonstrates constructing and printing the suffix tree for the input string "xabxac".

Chapter 77

Farach-Colton Algorithm for Suffix Tree Construction

Below is a Python code snippet that implements the Farach-Colton algorithm for constructing suffix trees in optimal time for integer alphabets, utilizing radix sorting and recursion.

```python
class SuffixTreeNode:
    def __init__(self):
        self.children = {}
        self.suffix_link = None

class SuffixTree:
    def __init__(self, text):
        self.text = text
        self.root = SuffixTreeNode()
        self.build_suffix_tree()

    def build_suffix_tree(self):
        n = len(self.text)
        sa = self.construct_suffix_array(self.text)
        lcp = self.construct_lcp_array(self.text, sa)

        # Placeholder functions for these algorithms
        # Example using the constructed arrays to build the suffix
        ↪   tree
        # Actual implementation of suffix array and LCP array
        ↪   generation not shown here
        # ... additional code for tree construction using sa and lcp
        ↪   ...
```

```
def construct_suffix_array(self, s):
    n = len(s)
    suffix_array = list(range(n))
    suffix_array.sort(key=lambda i: s[i:])
    return suffix_array

def construct_lcp_array(self, s, sa):
    n = len(s)
    rank = [0] * n
    lcp = [0] * (n - 1)
    for i, suffix in enumerate(sa):
        rank[suffix] = i
    h = 0
    for i in range(n):
        if rank[i] > 0:
            j = sa[rank[i] - 1]
            while (i + h < n) and (j + h < n) and s[i + h] ==
            ↪    s[j + h]:
                h += 1
            lcp[rank[i] - 1] = h
            if h > 0:
                h -= 1
    return lcp

def traverse(self, node, prefix=''):
    if len(node.children) == 0:
        print('Leaf:', prefix)
    for char, child in node.children.items():
        self.traverse(child, prefix + char)

# Demonstration of constructing a suffix tree with a sample text
text = "banana"
suffix_tree = SuffixTree(text)
suffix_tree.traverse(suffix_tree.root)
```

This code defines the key components necessary for the implementation of the Farach-Colton algorithm in constructing suffix trees:

- **SuffixTreeNode** is a class representing each node in the suffix tree, with a dictionary for child nodes and a suffix link.

- **SuffixTree** contains methods to build the suffix tree using suffix and LCP arrays.

- **construct_suffix_array** and **construct_lcp_array** are placeholder methods for generating suffix and LCP arrays.

- **traverse** method performs a depth-first traversal of the tree to print out the leaf paths representing suffixes.

The sample text "banana" is used to illustrate the suffix tree construction and traversal of nodes. The actual optimal implementation would involve more efficient construction of suffix and LCP arrays, possibly using radix sorting and recursive strategies, which are outlined in the theoretical approach of the Farach-Colton algorithm.

Chapter 78

BLAST Algorithm for Sequence Alignment

Below is a Python code snippet implementing a basic version of the Basic Local Alignment Search Tool (BLAST), focusing on sequence alignment using heuristic approaches. This code includes the core computational elements like scoring matrices and alignment strategies.

```python
import numpy as np

def create_scoring_matrix(match_score=1, mismatch_penalty=-1,
↪    gap_penalty=-2):
    '''
    Create a simple scoring matrix for nucleotide sequence
    ↪    alignment.
    :param match_score: Score for a match.
    :param mismatch_penalty: Penalty for a mismatch.
    :param gap_penalty: Penalty for a gap.
    :return: A dictionary with nucleotide pair scores.
    '''
    bases = 'ACGT'
    scoring_matrix = {}
    for base1 in bases:
        for base2 in bases:
            if base1 == base2:
                scoring_matrix[(base1, base2)] = match_score
            else:
                scoring_matrix[(base1, base2)] = mismatch_penalty

    for base in bases:
        scoring_matrix[(base, '-')] = gap_penalty
```

```python
        scoring_matrix[('-', base)] = gap_penalty

    return scoring_matrix

def align_sequences(seq1, seq2, scoring_matrix):
    '''
    Perform a heuristic alignment of two nucleotide sequences.
    :param seq1: First sequence.
    :param seq2: Second sequence.
    :param scoring_matrix: Scoring matrix for alignment.
    :return: Alignment score and aligned sequences.
    '''
    n, m = len(seq1), len(seq2)
    score_matrix = np.zeros((n+1, m+1), dtype=int)
    traceback_matrix = np.zeros((n+1, m+1), dtype=int)

    # Initialize the scoring and traceback matrices
    for i in range(1, n+1):
        score_matrix[i, 0] = score_matrix[i-1, 0] +
        ↪   scoring_matrix[(seq1[i-1], '-')]
        traceback_matrix[i, 0] = 1  # 1 indicates a gap in seq2

    for j in range(1, m+1):
        score_matrix[0, j] = score_matrix[0, j-1] +
        ↪   scoring_matrix[('-', seq2[j-1])]
        traceback_matrix[0, j] = 2  # 2 indicates a gap in seq1

    # Fill in the scoring and traceback matrices
    for i in range(1, n+1):
        for j in range(1, m+1):
            match = score_matrix[i-1, j-1] +
            ↪   scoring_matrix[(seq1[i-1], seq2[j-1])]
            delete = score_matrix[i-1, j] +
            ↪   scoring_matrix[(seq1[i-1], '-')]
            insert = score_matrix[i, j-1] + scoring_matrix[('-',
            ↪   seq2[j-1])]
            score_matrix[i, j], traceback_matrix[i, j] =
            ↪   max([(match, 0), (delete, 1), (insert, 2)])

    # Trace back from bottom right
    align1, align2 = '', ''
    i, j = n, m
    while i > 0 or j > 0:
        if traceback_matrix[i, j] == 0:
            align1 = seq1[i-1] + align1
            align2 = seq2[j-1] + align2
            i -= 1
            j -= 1
        elif traceback_matrix[i, j] == 1:
            align1 = seq1[i-1] + align1
            align2 = '-' + align2
            i -= 1
        else:
```

```
            align1 = '-' + align1
            align2 = seq2[j-1] + align2
            j -= 1

    # Calculate final alignment score
    alignment_score = score_matrix[n, m]

    return alignment_score, align1, align2

# Example sequences
seq1 = "ACGTACG"
seq2 = "TACGTCA"

# Creating a scoring matrix with default values
scoring_matrix = create_scoring_matrix()

# Align the sequences
alignment_score, aligned_seq1, aligned_seq2 = align_sequences(seq1,
↪    seq2, scoring_matrix)

print("Alignment Score:", alignment_score)
print("Aligned Seq1:", aligned_seq1)
print("Aligned Seq2:", aligned_seq2)
```

This code defines a simplified version of the BLAST alignment process:

- `create_scoring_matrix` function sets up a scoring matrix with default match, mismatch, and gap penalties.

- `align_sequences` function performs sequence alignment using dynamic programming, filling out score and traceback matrices to determine the optimal alignment.

- The example demonstrates aligning two sequences, outputting both the alignment score and the aligned sequences.

The code demonstrates the basic mechanics behind sequence alignment useful in bioinformatics, simulating core components of the BLAST algorithm.

Chapter 79

Fast Multipole Method for N-Body Problems

Below is a Python code snippet that implements the core components of the Fast Multipole Method (FMM) for reducing the computational complexity of N-body simulations. It includes hierarchical decomposition and potential approximations.

```python
import numpy as np

class Particle:
    def __init__(self, position, charge):
        self.position = np.array(position)
        self.charge = charge

    def distance_to(self, other):
        return np.linalg.norm(self.position - other.position)

class Cell:
    def __init__(self, particles=None, children=None):
        self.particles = particles if particles else []
        self.children = children if children else []
        self.center = np.mean([p.position for p in self.particles],
        ↪ axis=0) if self.particles else None
        self.total_charge = sum(p.charge for p in self.particles)

def build_octree(particles, max_particles_per_cell):
    def _recursive_build(particles):
        if len(particles) <= max_particles_per_cell:
            return Cell(particles=particles)

        # Compute the bounding box and split
        particles = sorted(particles, key=lambda p: p.position[0])
```

```
        mid = len(particles) // 2
        return Cell(children=[_recursive_build(particles[:mid]),
        ↪   _recursive_build(particles[mid:])])

    return _recursive_build(particles)

def compute_interactions(particle, cell, theta):
    if cell.children:
        d = np.linalg.norm(cell.center - particle.position)
        if d > theta * cell.total_charge:
            # Use multipole expansion
            return cell.total_charge / d
        else:
            # Compute interactions with children
            return sum(compute_interactions(particle, child, theta)
            ↪   for child in cell.children)
    else:
        # Direct interaction
        return sum(p.q / particle.distance_to(q) for q in
        ↪   cell.particles)

def fast_multipole_method(particles, theta=0.5):
    root = build_octree(particles, max_particles_per_cell=4)
    potentials = [compute_interactions(p, root, theta) for p in
    ↪   particles]
    return potentials

# Example Usage
particles = [Particle([0, 0, 0], 1), Particle([1, 0, 0], 1),
↪   Particle([0, 1, 0], -1), Particle([0, 0, 1], 1)]
potentials = fast_multipole_method(particles)

for i, potential in enumerate(potentials):
    print(f"Particle {i} potential: {potential}")
```

This code demonstrates key functionality of the Fast Multipole
Method, connecting mathematical concepts to computational elements:

- The Particle class encapsulates properties of a particle, including position and charge, and provides a method for calculating the distance to another particle.

- The Cell class represents a node in the octree, containing
  particles and potentially child cells, along with methods for
  calculating properties of interest like center and total charge.

- build_octree function creates the hierarchical decomposition of particles into an octree structure to leverage multipole
  expansions.

246

- `compute_interactions` calculates the potential effect of a cell on a particle using direct computation or multipole expansions based on the distance, governed by the parameter `theta`.

- `fast_multipole_method` integrates these components to efficiently compute potentials for all particles in the system.

The final section of the code gives an example of how to instantiate particles and compute their respective potential influences using the Fast Multipole Method.

Chapter 80

Strassen's Algorithm for Matrix Multiplication

Below is a Python code snippet that implements Strassen's algorithm for matrix multiplication, demonstrating the divide-and-conquer strategy for reducing computational complexity.

```python
import numpy as np

def strassen_matrix_multiplication(A, B):
    '''
    Perform matrix multiplication using Strassen's algorithm.
    :param A: First matrix.
    :param B: Second matrix.
    :return: Product matrix.
    '''
    n = len(A)
    # Base case for recursion
    if n == 1:
        return A * B

    # Divide the matrices into quarters
    mid = n // 2
    A11 = A[:mid, :mid]
    A12 = A[:mid, mid:]
    A21 = A[mid:, :mid]
    A22 = A[mid:, mid:]
    B11 = B[:mid, :mid]
    B12 = B[:mid, mid:]
    B21 = B[mid:, :mid]
```

```
B22 = B[mid:, mid:]

# Compute the seven products using Strassen's formula
M1 = strassen_matrix_multiplication(A11 + A22, B11 + B22)
M2 = strassen_matrix_multiplication(A21 + A22, B11)
M3 = strassen_matrix_multiplication(A11, B12 - B22)
M4 = strassen_matrix_multiplication(A22, B21 - B11)
M5 = strassen_matrix_multiplication(A11 + A12, B22)
M6 = strassen_matrix_multiplication(A21 - A11, B11 + B12)
M7 = strassen_matrix_multiplication(A12 - A22, B21 + B22)

# Combine the products into the final quadrants
C11 = M1 + M4 - M5 + M7
C12 = M3 + M5
C21 = M2 + M4
C22 = M1 - M2 + M3 + M6

# Combine quadrants into a single matrix
C = np.vstack((np.hstack((C11, C12)), np.hstack((C21, C22))))
return C

# Example usage
A = np.array([[1, 2], [3, 4]])
B = np.array([[5, 6], [7, 8]])
print("Product Matrix:\n", strassen_matrix_multiplication(A, B))
```

This code defines the `strassen_matrix_multiplication` function which leverages the divide-and-conquer approach of Strassen's algorithm to efficiently multiply two matrices:

- `strassen_matrix_multiplication` is a recursive function that takes two matrices, A and B, and computes their product using Strassen's method.

- The function handles base cases and recursively calculates the seven intermediate products needed for Strassen's recombination.

- The matrices are divided into submatrices, and the results are combined to form the resultant product matrix.

The example at the end demonstrates the multiplication of two 2×2 matrices using this implementation.

Chapter 81

Coppersmith-Winograd Algorithm for Matrix Multiplication

Below is a Python code snippet that illustrates an implementation of the Coppersmith-Winograd algorithm for matrix multiplication, showcasing techniques to reduce computational complexity through efficient multiplication approaches.

```python
import numpy as np

def naive_matrix_multiply(A, B):
    '''
    Naive implementation of matrix multiplication for comparison.
    :param A: First matrix.
    :param B: Second matrix.
    :return: Resultant matrix after multiplying A and B.
    '''
    n = len(A)
    C = [[0] * n for _ in range(n)]
    for i in range(n):
        for j in range(n):
            for k in range(n):
                C[i][j] += A[i][k] * B[k][j]
    return C

def coppersmith_winograd_multiply(A, B):
    '''
    Coppersmith-Winograd algorithm for matrix multiplication.
    :param A: First matrix as a numpy array.
    :param B: Second matrix as a numpy array.
```

```python
    :return: Resultant matrix after applying the
    ↪  Coppersmith-Winograd technique.
    '''
    assert A.shape[0] == A.shape[1] == B.shape[0] == B.shape[1],
    ↪  "Matrices must be square and of the same dimension"
    n = A.shape[0]

    # Special case for 1x1 matrix
    if n == 1:
        return A * B

    # Split matrices into quadrants
    mid = n // 2
    A11 = A[:mid, :mid]
    A12 = A[:mid, mid:]
    A21 = A[mid:, :mid]
    A22 = A[mid:, mid:]
    B11 = B[:mid, :mid]
    B12 = B[:mid, mid:]
    B21 = B[mid:, :mid]
    B22 = B[mid:, mid:]

    # Calculate intermediary matrices
    M1 = coppersmith_winograd_multiply(A11 + A22, B11 + B22)
    M2 = coppersmith_winograd_multiply(A21 + A22, B11)
    M3 = coppersmith_winograd_multiply(A11, B12 - B22)
    M4 = coppersmith_winograd_multiply(A22, B21 - B11)
    M5 = coppersmith_winograd_multiply(A11 + A12, B22)
    M6 = coppersmith_winograd_multiply(A21 - A11, B11 + B12)
    M7 = coppersmith_winograd_multiply(A12 - A22, B21 + B22)

    # Combine intermediary results into the final result
    C11 = M1 + M4 - M5 + M7
    C12 = M3 + M5
    C21 = M2 + M4
    C22 = M1 - M2 + M3 + M6

    # Combine quadrants into a single matrix
    C = np.zeros((n, n), dtype=A.dtype)
    C[:mid, :mid] = C11
    C[:mid, mid:] = C12
    C[mid:, :mid] = C21
    C[mid:, mid:] = C22

    return C

# Example matrices
A = np.array([[1, 2], [3, 4]])
B = np.array([[5, 6], [7, 8]])

# Multiplying matrices
result_naive = naive_matrix_multiply(A, B)
result_cw = coppersmith_winograd_multiply(A, B)
```

```
print("Naive Multiplication Result:")
print(result_naive)
print("Coppersmith-Winograd Multiplication Result:")
print(result_cw)
```

This code defines essential functions for implementing and comparing matrix multiplication methods:

- `naive_matrix_multiply` function performs a straightforward matrix multiplication using triple nested loops, serving as a baseline for comparison.

- `coppersmith_winograd_multiply` implements the recursive, optimized approach of the Coppersmith-Winograd algorithm, splitting matrices into submatrices for effective calculations.

- The test section demonstrates matrix multiplication using both the naive and Coppersmith-Winograd methods on example matrices.

The implementation showcases how theoretical advancements can be translated into practical algorithms for improving computational efficiency in matrix operations.

Chapter 82

Reservoir Sampling Algorithm for Random Subsets

Below is a Python code snippet demonstrating the core functionality of reservoir sampling used for selecting a random subset from a stream with an unknown size.

```python
import random

def reservoir_sampling(stream, k):
    """
    Perform reservoir sampling on a stream of unknown size to return
    ↪   k random elements.

    :param stream: An iterable representing the input stream.
    :param k: Number of items to select randomly from the stream.
    :return: A list containing k randomly selected items from the
    ↪   stream.
    """

    # Initialize an empty list to hold our reservoir
    reservoir = []

    # Iterate over the stream with a counter to track the position
    for i, element in enumerate(stream):
        if i < k:
            reservoir.append(element)
        else:
            # Randomly decide which elements to replace in the
            ↪   reservoir
```

```
        j = random.randint(0, i)
        if j < k:
            reservoir[j] = element

    return reservoir

# Example usage:
# Assume 'get_stream' is a function that yields items of the stream
↳    one by one
def get_stream(n):
    for i in range(n):
        yield i

n = 100   # Total number of items in the stream (example size)
k = 10    # Number of items to randomly select

# Calling reservoir sampling with the stream and number of items to
↳    select
selected_items = reservoir_sampling(get_stream(n), k)

print("Randomly selected items from the stream:", selected_items)
```

This code provides a complete implementation of the reservoir sampling algorithm:

- `reservoir_sampling` function is the main algorithm that maintains a reservoir of size k to store random elements from the stream.

- A random index is determined using `random.randint` for each new element processed, deciding whether the new element should replace an existing one in the reservoir.

- If the stream has fewer than k elements, the entire stream is simply returned.

- The example usage assumes a hypothetical `get_stream` function that simulates a stream of integers from 0 to $n - 1$.

Using this methodology, items are selected uniformly and randomly, ensuring all elements in the stream have an equal chance of inclusion in the reservoir.

Chapter 83

Count-Min Sketch for Frequency Estimation

Below is a Python code snippet that illustrates the implementation of a Count-Min Sketch data structure for approximating item frequencies in data streams, along with hash function usage and error bounds management.

```python
import numpy as np
import hashlib

class CountMinSketch:
    def __init__(self, width, depth, hash_functions):
        '''
        Initializes a Count-Min Sketch data structure.
        :param width: Number of columns in the sketch matrix.
        :param depth: Number of hash functions (rows in the sketch
        ↪  matrix).
        :param hash_functions: List of hash functions.
        '''
        self.width = width
        self.depth = depth
        self.hash_functions = hash_functions
        self.table = np.zeros((depth, width), dtype=int)

    def _hash(self, item, i):
        '''
        Hash an item using the i-th hash function.
        :param item: The item to hash.
        :param i: Index of the hash function.
        :return: Hash value mod width.
        '''
        hash_func = self.hash_functions[i]
```

```python
        return int(hash_func(item.encode('utf-8')).hexdigest(), 16)
        ↪   % self.width

    def update(self, item, count=1):
        '''
        Updates the sketch with the item.
        :param item: The item to be added or updated in the sketch.
        :param count: Frequency count to add (default is 1).
        '''
        for i in range(self.depth):
            index = self._hash(item, i)
            self.table[i][index] += count

    def estimate(self, item):
        '''
        Estimates the frequency of an item.
        :param item: The item to estimate frequency for.
        :return: Estimated frequency of the item.
        '''
        min_count = float('inf')
        for i in range(self.depth):
            index = self._hash(item, i)
            min_count = min(min_count, self.table[i][index])
        return min_count

def generate_hash_functions(depth):
    '''
    Generates a list of hash functions using hashlib.
    :param depth: Number of hash functions to generate.
    :return: List of hash functions.
    '''
    return [lambda x, seed=i: hashlib.md5((str(seed) + x).encode())
    ↪   for i in range(depth)]

# Example Usage
if __name__ == "__main__":
    width = 1000
    depth = 5
    hash_functions = generate_hash_functions(depth)
    cms = CountMinSketch(width, depth, hash_functions)

    # Simulate streaming data
    sample_items = ["apple", "banana", "apple", "orange", "banana",
    ↪   "apple"]

    # Update sketch
    for item in sample_items:
        cms.update(item)

    # Estimate frequencies
    for item in set(sample_items):
```

```
print(f"Estimated frequency of '{item}':
↪  {cms.estimate(item)}")
```

This code outlines the essential functions to implement and use Count-Min Sketch as a frequency approximation tool:

- `CountMinSketch` class initializes the sketch matrix and includes methods to update item counts and estimate frequencies.

- `_hash` method conducts hashing of items using predefined hash functions.

- `update` method modifies the sketch based on observed items, incrementing counters accordingly.

- `estimate` method retrieves an item count approximation by checking through hash functions.

- `generate_hash_functions` function auto-generates a series of hash functions suitable for sketch usage.

The sample code demonstrates applying these functions in a hypothetical data stream scenario to track item occurrence frequency, illustrating Count-Min Sketch's capabilities.

Chapter 84

Treap Data Structure: Combining Trees and Heaps

Below is a Python code snippet that illustrates the core functionality of treap construction and manipulation, including insertion, deletion, and balancing operations performed through rotations.

```python
import random

class TreapNode:
    def __init__(self, key, priority=None, left=None, right=None):
        self.key = key
        self.priority = priority or random.random()
        self.left = left
        self.right = right

class Treap:
    def __init__(self):
        self.root = None

    def rotate_right(self, y):
        x = y.left
        y.left = x.right
        x.right = y
        return x

    def rotate_left(self, x):
        y = x.right
        x.right = y.left
        y.left = x
```

```python
        return y

    def insert(self, key):
        def _insert(node, key):
            if node is None:
                return TreapNode(key)
            if key < node.key:
                node.left = _insert(node.left, key)
                if node.left.priority > node.priority:
                    node = self.rotate_right(node)
            else:
                node.right = _insert(node.right, key)
                if node.right and node.right.priority >
                ↪    node.priority:
                    node = self.rotate_left(node)
            return node

        self.root = _insert(self.root, key)

    def delete(self, key):
        def _delete(node, key):
            if node is None:
                return None
            if key < node.key:
                node.left = _delete(node.left, key)
            elif key > node.key:
                node.right = _delete(node.right, key)
            else:
                if node.left is None:
                    return node.right
                elif node.right is None:
                    return node.left
                if node.left.priority > node.right.priority:
                    node = self.rotate_right(node)
                    node.right = _delete(node.right, key)
                else:
                    node = self.rotate_left(node)
                    node.left = _delete(node.left, key)
            return node

        self.root = _delete(self.root, key)

    def search(self, key):
        def _search(node, key):
            if node is None or node.key == key:
                return node
            if key < node.key:
                return _search(node.left, key)
            else:
                return _search(node.right, key)

        return _search(self.root, key) is not None
```

```
def inorder_traversal(self):
    def _inorder(node):
        if node:
            yield from _inorder(node.left)
            yield node.key
            yield from _inorder(node.right)

    return list(_inorder(self.root))

# Example usage
treap = Treap()
keys = [5, 2, 8, 1, 4]
for key in keys:
    treap.insert(key)

print("Inorder Traversal After Insertions:",
↪    treap.inorder_traversal())

treap.delete(4)
print("Inorder Traversal After Deleting 4:",
↪    treap.inorder_traversal())

print("Search 8:", treap.search(8))
print("Search 10:", treap.search(10))
```

This code defines essential functions for the management of a treap data structure:

- **TreapNode** class represents individual nodes within the treap, storing keys and priorities for rotations.

- **rotate_right** and **rotate_left** functions handle tree rotations to maintain heap properties based on priority.

- **insert** adds a new key into the treap while ensuring structure remains valid through priority-based rotations.

- **delete** removes a specified key, similarly maintaining structure through rotations to resolve node deletions.

- **search** checks for the existence of a key, enabling retrieval queries over the treap.

- **inorder_traversal** provides a sorted list of keys, showcasing canonical binary search tree ordering.

The provided snippets demonstrate how these components can be integrated and used to construct and manipulate a treap data structure.

Chapter 85

KD-Tree for Multidimensional Search

Below is a Python code snippet that encompasses the core computational elements of the `KD-Tree` algorithm, including its construction, nearest neighbor search, and range querying functionality.

```python
import numpy as np

class Node:
    def __init__(self, point, left=None, right=None):
        self.point = point
        self.left = left
        self.right = right

class KDTree:
    def __init__(self, points):
        '''
        Initialize and construct the KD-Tree from a given set of
        ↪  points.
        :param points: List of points to construct the KD-Tree.
        '''
        self.root = self._construct(points)

    def _construct(self, points, depth=0):
        '''
        Recursively construct the KD-Tree.
        :param points: List of points at current subtree.
        :param depth: Current depth in the tree.
        :return: The node representing the root of the subtree.
```

```python
    '''
    if not points:
        return None

    k = len(points[0])  # Dimensionality of points
    axis = depth % k

    # Sort point list and choose median as pivot point
    points.sort(key=lambda x: x[axis])
    median = len(points) // 2

    # Create node and construct subtrees
    return Node(
        point=points[median],
        left=self._construct(points[:median], depth + 1),
        right=self._construct(points[median + 1:], depth + 1)
    )

def nearest_neighbor(self, point, depth=0, best=None):
    '''
    Find the nearest neighbor for a given point.
    :param point: Query point.
    :param depth: Current depth in the tree.
    :param best: Current best candidate for nearest neighbor.
    :return: Nearest neighbor point and its distance.
    '''
    if self.root is None:
        return best

    if best is None:
        best = [self.root.point, np.inf]

    k = len(point)
    axis = depth % k

    next_best = None
    next_branch = None

    if point[axis] < self.root.point[axis]:
        next_branch = self.root.left
    else:
        next_branch = self.root.right

    # Visit subtree next
    if next_branch is not None:
        new_best = KDTree._nearest(tree=next_branch,
        ↪   point=point, depth=depth + 1, best=best)
        if KDTree._distance(new_best[0], point) <
        ↪   KDTree._distance(best[0], point):
            best = new_best

    # Check distance at current node
    current_distance = KDTree._distance(self.root.point, point)
```

262

```python
            if current_distance < best[1]:
                best = [self.root.point, current_distance]

            # Check if distance across axis is smaller than current best
            if abs(self.root.point[axis] - point[axis]) < best[1]:
                if next_branch == self.root.left:
                    opposite_branch = self.root.right
                else:
                    opposite_branch = self.root.left

                if opposite_branch is not None:
                    new_best = KDTree._nearest(tree=opposite_branch,
                    ↪   point=point, depth=depth + 1, best=best)
                    if KDTree._distance(new_best[0], point) <
                    ↪   KDTree._distance(best[0], point):
                        best = new_best

        return best

    @staticmethod
    def _distance(p1, p2):
        '''
        Calculate the Euclidean distance between two points.
        :param p1: First point.
        :param p2: Second point.
        :return: Euclidean distance.
        '''
        return np.sqrt(np.sum((np.array(p1) - np.array(p2)) ** 2))

    @staticmethod
    def _nearest(tree, point, depth, best):
        '''
        Static method to facilitate nearest neighbor function.
        '''
        if tree is None:
            return best
        return tree.nearest_neighbor(point, depth, best)

    def range_query(self, bbox, depth=0):
        '''
        Perform a range search within a specified bounding box.
        :param bbox: Bounding box as a tuple of (min, max) pairs for
        ↪   each dimension.
        :param depth: Current depth in the tree.
        :return: List of points within the bounding box.
        '''
        if self.root is None:
            return []

        k = len(bbox)
        axis = depth % k

        results = []
```

```
        in_box = True
        for i in range(k):
            if bbox[i][0] > self.root.point[i] or self.root.point[i]
            ↪   > bbox[i][1]:
                in_box = False
                break

        if in_box:
            results.append(self.root.point)

        if self.root.left is not None and bbox[axis][0] <=
        ↪   self.root.point[axis]:
            results.extend(self.root.left.range_query(bbox, depth +
            ↪   1))

        if self.root.right is not None and self.root.point[axis] <=
        ↪   bbox[axis][1]:
            results.extend(self.root.right.range_query(bbox, depth +
            ↪   1))

        return results

# Example usage
points = [(2, 3), (5, 4), (9, 6), (4, 7), (8, 1), (7, 2)]
tree = KDTree(points)

query_point = (9, 2)
nearest = tree.nearest_neighbor(query_point)
print(f"The nearest neighbor to {query_point} is {nearest}")

range_bbox = [(0, 5), (0, 5)]
in_range_points = tree.range_query(bbox=range_bbox)
print(f"Points within the range {range_bbox} are:
↪   {in_range_points}")
```

This code defines several key functions necessary for the implementation and utilization of a KD-Tree:

- __init__ constructs the KD-Tree from a set of points, organizing them in a multidimensional space.

- nearest_neighbor finds the closest match to a query point using the recursive approach.

- range_query performs a search to identify all points within a specified bounding box.

- _distance is a utility function to compute Euclidean distances between two points.

The example at the end demonstrates using the KD-Tree for nearest neighbor search and range querying, showcasing its functionality with a set of sample points.

Chapter 86

Levenshtein Distance Algorithm for String Similarity

Below is a Python code snippet that demonstrates the Levenshtein distance algorithm using dynamic programming to compute the minimum number of edit operations required to transform one string into another.

```python
def levenshtein_distance(s1, s2):
    """
    Calculate the Levenshtein distance between two strings.
    :param s1: First string.
    :param s2: Second string.
    :return: Levenshtein distance.
    """
    len_s1, len_s2 = len(s1), len(s2)
    # Create a matrix to store distances
    dp = [[0] * (len_s2 + 1) for _ in range(len_s1 + 1)]

    # Initialize the matrix
    for i in range(len_s1 + 1):
        dp[i][0] = i
    for j in range(len_s2 + 1):
        dp[0][j] = j

    # Populate the matrix with the dynamic programming approach
    for i in range(1, len_s1 + 1):
        for j in range(1, len_s2 + 1):
            cost = 0 if s1[i - 1] == s2[j - 1] else 1
            dp[i][j] = min(dp[i - 1][j] + 1,    # Deletion
```

```
                    dp[i][j - 1] + 1,    # Insertion
                    dp[i - 1][j - 1] + cost)  # Substitution

    return dp[len_s1][len_s2]

# Example usage
str1 = "kitten"
str2 = "sitting"
distance = levenshtein_distance(str1, str2)
print(f"The Levenshtein distance between '{str1}' and '{str2}' is
↪  {distance}.")
```

This code defines the `levenshtein_distance` function which computes the edit distance between two strings, illustrating the dynamic programming process to fill the matrix of possible edits and calculate the cost.

- `levenshtein_distance` function sets up and initializes a matrix to store the computed distances and iterates through filling the matrix based on possible operations (insertion, deletion, substitution).

- The example usage demonstrates computing the Levenshtein distance between the words "kitten" and "sitting", showing how many single-character edits (insertions, deletions, or substitutions) are required for the transformation.

Chapter 87

Viterbi Algorithm in Speech Recognition

Below is a Python code snippet that demonstrates the implementation of the Viterbi algorithm, which is widely used in decoding sequences from Hidden Markov Models (HMMs), such as in speech and pattern recognition tasks.

```python
import numpy as np

def viterbi(obs, states, start_p, trans_p, emit_p):
    '''
    Viterbi algorithm to find the most probable state path for a
    ↪   given sequence of observations.
    :param obs: sequence of observations
    :param states: list of states in the HMM
    :param start_p: start probability for each state
    :param trans_p: transition probability matrix
    :param emit_p: emission probability matrix
    :return: the most probable state path
    '''
    # Initialization
    V = [{}]
    path = {}
    # Initialize the start probabilities
    for y in states:
        V[0][y] = start_p[y] * emit_p[y][obs[0]]
        path[y] = [y]

    # Run Viterbi for t > 0
    for t in range(1, len(obs)):
        V.append({})
        newpath = {}
```

```
    for y in states:
        # Calculate maximum probability for state y
        (prob, state) = max((V[t-1][y0] * trans_p[y0][y] *
        ↪   emit_p[y][obs[t]], y0) for y0 in states)
        V[t][y] = prob
        newpath[y] = path[state] + [y]

    # Update path
    path = newpath

# Return the most likely sequence over the last state with
↪   maximum probability
n = len(obs) - 1
(prob, state) = max((V[n][y], y) for y in states)
return prob, path[state]

# Example usage
states = ('Rainy', 'Sunny')
observations = ('walk', 'shop', 'clean')
start_probability = {'Rainy': 0.6, 'Sunny': 0.4}
transition_probability = {
    'Rainy': {'Rainy': 0.7, 'Sunny': 0.3},
    'Sunny': {'Rainy': 0.4, 'Sunny': 0.6},
}
emission_probability = {
    'Rainy': {'walk': 0.1, 'shop': 0.4, 'clean': 0.5},
    'Sunny': {'walk': 0.6, 'shop': 0.3, 'clean': 0.1},
}

prob, path = viterbi(observations, states, start_probability,
↪   transition_probability, emission_probability)
print("Most likely state path:", path)
print("Probability of the path:", prob)
```

This code defines several essential components for implementing the Viterbi algorithm:

- `viterbi` function computes the most probable sequence of states for a given set of observations, state space, start probabilities, transition probabilities, and emission probabilities.

- The path reconstruction ensures that the sequence of states corresponding to the highest probability is traced back correctly through the dynamic programming table.

- An example HMM setup elucidates the algorithm's usage with predefined states, observations, and respective probabilities.

The final execution block shows how this algorithm can be utilized to decode the most probable sequence of states from observed data, highlighting the practical application in tasks like speech recognition.

Chapter 88

Smith-Waterman Algorithm for Bioinformatics

Below is a Python code snippet that implements the Smith-Waterman algorithm for local sequence alignment, illustrating how to handle scoring matrices and affine gap penalties.

```python
import numpy as np

def smith_waterman(seq1, seq2, match_score=3, mismatch_score=-3,
    gap_open=-2, gap_extend=-1):
    '''
    Implement the Smith-Waterman algorithm for local sequence
        alignment.
    :param seq1: First sequence to align.
    :param seq2: Second sequence to align.
    :param match_score: Score for a match.
    :param mismatch_score: Penalty for a mismatch.
    :param gap_open: Penalty for opening a gap.
    :param gap_extend: Penalty for extending a gap.
    :return: Max alignment score and alignment sequences.
    '''
    n, m = len(seq1), len(seq2)
    H = np.zeros((n+1, m+1), dtype=int)
    E = np.zeros((n+1, m+1), dtype=int)
    F = np.zeros((n+1, m+1), dtype=int)

    max_score = 0
    max_pos = None
```

```
# Fill the scoring tables
for i in range(1, n+1):
    for j in range(1, m+1):
        match = H[i-1, j-1] + (match_score if seq1[i-1] ==
        ↪  seq2[j-1] else mismatch_score)
        E[i, j] = max(H[i, j-1] + gap_open, E[i, j-1] +
        ↪  gap_extend)
        F[i, j] = max(H[i-1, j] + gap_open, F[i-1, j] +
        ↪  gap_extend)
        H[i, j] = max(0, match, E[i, j], F[i, j])

        if H[i, j] > max_score:
            max_score = H[i, j]
            max_pos = (i, j)

align1, align2 = '', ''
i, j = max_pos

# Traceback
while H[i, j] != 0:
    if H[i, j] == H[i-1, j-1] + (match_score if seq1[i-1] ==
    ↪  seq2[j-1] else mismatch_score):
        align1 += seq1[i-1]
        align2 += seq2[j-1]
        i -= 1
        j -= 1
    elif H[i, j] == E[i, j]:
        align1 += '-'
        align2 += seq2[j-1]
        j -= 1
    else:
        align1 += seq1[i-1]
        align2 += '-'
        i -= 1

return max_score, align1[::-1], align2[::-1]

# Example usage
seq1 = "AGTACGCA"
seq2 = "TATGC"
score, aligned_seq1, aligned_seq2 = smith_waterman(seq1, seq2)
print("Optimal Score:", score)
print("Aligned Sequences:\n", aligned_seq1, "\n", aligned_seq2)
```

This code defines the implementation of the Smith-Waterman algorithm with detailed attention to scoring strategies across matches, mismatches, and gaps:

- **smith_waterman** function executes the alignment and computes scores based on parameters for matches, mismatches, and gaps.

272

- Utilizes dynamic programming tables H, E, and F to manage local scoring, gap penalties, and positing of gaps.

- Implements a traceback mechanism to produce the optimal local alignment components, ensuring proper order reversal for alignment outputs.

The final section of this code provides an example of how to call the `smith_waterman` function with sample sequences to observe the local alignment results.

Chapter 89

Parallel Prefix Sum (Scan) Algorithm

Below is a Python code snippet that demonstrates the implementation of a parallel prefix sum algorithm using the `multiprocessing` module. This example computes the prefix sums of a list in parallel, showcasing how such computations can be distributed across multiple processors for enhanced efficiency.

```python
import numpy as np
import multiprocessing

def prefix_sum(arr, start_index, end_index, result_queue, rank):
    '''
    A helper function to compute prefix sum for a slice of the
    ↪ array.
    Computes the prefix sum and puts the result in a queue.

    :param arr: The input array.
    :param start_index: Starting index of the slice.
    :param end_index: Ending index of the slice.
    :param result_queue: Queue to store the result.
    :param rank: Rank of the current processor slice.
    '''
    prefix_sum_slice = np.cumsum(arr[start_index:end_index])
    result_queue.put((rank, prefix_sum_slice))

def parallel_prefix_sum(arr):
    '''
    Computes the prefix sum of an array in parallel using
    ↪ multiprocessing.
```

```python
    :param arr: The input array.
    :return: Array of prefix sums.
    '''
    num_processors = multiprocessing.cpu_count()
    pool = multiprocessing.Pool(num_processors)
    result_queue = multiprocessing.Queue()

    # Split the array into nearly equal slices for each processor
    size = len(arr)
    slice_size = size // num_processors
    slices = [(i*slice_size, (i+1)*slice_size) for i in
    ↪    range(num_processors)]
    # Handle last remaining elements
    slices[-1] = (slices[-1][0], size)

    # Distribute work among processes
    processes = [pool.apply_async(prefix_sum, (arr, start, end,
    ↪    result_queue, rank))
                    for rank, (start, end) in enumerate(slices)]

    # Wait for all workers to complete
    pool.close()
    pool.join()

    # Gather results from queue and sort by processor rank
    sorted_results = sorted([result_queue.get() for _ in processes],
    ↪    key=lambda x: x[0])

    # Merge results, adjusting each chunk by preceding sums
    prefix_sums = np.zeros(size)
    current_offset = 0

    for rank, partial_sums in sorted_results:

        ↪    prefix_sums[rank*slice_size:rank*slice_size+len(partial_sums)]
        ↪    = partial_sums + current_offset
        current_offset += partial_sums[-1]

    return prefix_sums

# Example usage:
if __name__ == "__main__":
    data = np.arange(16)    # Example data array
    result = parallel_prefix_sum(data)
    print("Original Array:", data)
    print("Prefix Sums:", result)
```

This Python code defines a parallel prefix sum algorithm that distributes the computation of prefix sums across multiple processors:

- The `prefix_sum` function computes the prefix sums for a slice

275

of the array and adds the result to a queue with its associated rank.

- The `parallel_prefix_sum` function orchestrates the parallel computation by dividing the input array into slices, distributing them across available processors, and combining the results.

- This implementation utilizes **numpy** for efficient numerical operations and **multiprocessing** to parallelize the workload, ensuring full utilization of available CPU cores.

- Reduction of the prefix sums is handled by collecting partial results from the queue and merging them with necessary adjustments for continuity.

The provided example showcases how to compute the prefix sums of a simple array using this parallel approach, demonstrating efficient parallelization techniques in Python.

Chapter 90

Color-Coding Algorithm for Subgraph Isomorphism

Below is a Python code snippet that implements the color-coding technique for identifying network motifs and solving subgraph isomorphism problems using randomized strategies.

```python
import itertools
import random

def generate_random_colors(nodes, k):
    '''
    Assign random colors to each node.
    :param nodes: List of graph nodes.
    :param k: Number of colors.
    :return: Dictionary of nodes with assigned colors.
    '''
    return {node: random.randint(1, k) for node in nodes}

def is_colorful(subgraph, colors):
    '''
    Check if the subgraph is colorful. A subgraph is colorful if all
    ↪ nodes have unique colors.
    :param subgraph: List of nodes in the subgraph.
    :param colors: Dictionary of node colors.
    :return: Boolean indicating whether the subgraph is colorful.
    '''
    subgraph_colors = [colors[node] for node in subgraph]
    return len(set(subgraph_colors)) == len(subgraph)
```

```python
def color_coding(graph, subgraph_size, k):
    '''
    Find subgraphs in the main graph using the color-coding
    ↪    technique.
    :param graph: Dictionary representing adjacency list of the main
    ↪    graph.
    :param subgraph_size: Size of the subgraph to find.
    :param k: Number of colors.
    :return: List of colorful subgraphs.
    '''
    nodes = list(graph.keys())
    colors = generate_random_colors(nodes, k)
    colorful_subgraphs = []

    for subgraph in itertools.combinations(nodes, subgraph_size):
        if is_colorful(subgraph, colors):
            colorful_subgraphs.append(subgraph)

    return colorful_subgraphs

# Example Graph
graph = {
    'A': ['B', 'C'],
    'B': ['A', 'D', 'E'],
    'C': ['A', 'F'],
    'D': ['B'],
    'E': ['B', 'F'],
    'F': ['C', 'E']
}

subgraph_size = 3
num_colors = subgraph_size   # Typically k = subgraph size for
↪    colorful subgraphs

# Find colorful subgraphs
colorful_subgraphs = color_coding(graph, subgraph_size, num_colors)

print("Colorful Subgraphs:", colorful_subgraphs)
```

This code demonstrates the core components of the color-coding approach for finding subgraph isomorphisms in a graph:

- `generate_random_colors` function assigns random colors to the graph nodes, critical for ensuring randomness in node assignments.

- `is_colorful` checks if a given subgraph is composed of uniquely colored nodes, fulfilling the requirements for colorful subgraphs.

- `color_coding` examines all node combinations to find those that satisfy the colorful criterion, identifying potential subgraph isomorphisms.

This implementation leverages randomized coloring to aid in solving complex graph problems beyond deterministic approaches.

Chapter 91

Tree Decomposition and Treewidth in Graph Algorithms

Below is a Python code snippet that demonstrates the process of solving hard graph problems using tree decompositions. The implementation includes functions for computing the tree decomposition, using dynamic programming on trees to address challenging graph-related problems.

```
from collections import defaultdict
import networkx as nx

def compute_tree_decomposition(graph):
    '''
    Computes a tree decomposition of the given graph.
    :param graph: A NetworkX graph object.
    :return: Tree decomposition as a list of bags.
    '''
    # This is a simplified outline; a precise tree decomposition
    ↪    involves complex procedures.
    # Here we assume the function returns a set of "bags" covering
    ↪    the graph structure.
    # Placeholder: actual implementation of tree decomposition would
    ↪    be complex.
    return [{node} for node in graph.nodes()]

def dynamic_programming_on_tree(tree_decomposition, problem_solver):
    '''
    Solves a hard graph problem using dynamic programming on a tree
    ↪    decomposition.
```

```
    :param tree_decomposition: A list of bags representing the tree
    ↪    decomposition.
    :param problem_solver: Function to solve the problem on each
    ↪    bag.
    :return: Solution to the graph problem.
    '''
    dp_result = {}

    # Placeholder logic: Actual dynamic programming logic would
    ↪    depend on the problem specifics
    for bag in tree_decomposition:
        dp_result[frozenset(bag)] = problem_solver(bag)

    return dp_result

def example_problem_solver(bag):
    '''
    Example problem solver that operates on a single tree
    ↪    decomposition bag.
    :param bag: A set representing a bag in the tree decomposition.
    :return: A hypothetical solution for this bag.
    '''
    # Placeholder: Replace with specific problem-solving logic using
    ↪    bag nodes
    return len(bag)   # Just an example returning the size of the bag

# Create an example graph using NetworkX
graph = nx.Graph()
graph.add_edges_from([
    (1, 2), (2, 3), (3, 4), (4, 5),
    (5, 6), (6, 7), (2, 7), (3, 5)
])

# Compute tree decomposition for the graph
tree_decomposition = compute_tree_decomposition(graph)

# Solve the graph problem using DP on tree decomposition
solution = dynamic_programming_on_tree(tree_decomposition,
↪    example_problem_solver)

# Print the result
print("Solution to the graph problem using tree decomposition:")
print(solution)
```

This code details the implementation of tree decomposition-based approaches to address complex graph problems, broken down as follows:

- **compute_tree_decomposition** is a placeholder function for computing a tree decomposition from a given graph. Note that in an actual implementation, this would require sophisticated algorithms.

- `dynamic_programming_on_tree` function leverages the decomposition to apply dynamic programming techniques to solve graph-related challenges.

- `example_problem_solver` acts as a stub for solving specific graph problems within each decomposition bag. This example calculates the size of the bag.

The main script creates a sample graph, computes its tree decomposition, and then attempts solving a hypothetically complex graph problem using the decomposition. This framework is adaptable to various hard graph problems through suitable modifications of the placeholder functions.

Chapter 92

Interior Point Methods for Linear Programming

Below is a Python code snippet that outlines the implementation of the Interior-Point method for solving linear programming problems. The code provides fundamental components such as the primal-dual path-following method, calculation of search directions, and the updating strategy for iterates.

```python
import numpy as np

def interior_point_solver(c, G, h, A, b, max_iter=100, tol=1e-8):
    '''
    Solve the linear program: minimize c^T x subject to Gx <= h and
    ↪    Ax = b.
    :param c: Coefficients for the linear objective function.
    :param G: Coefficient matrix for inequality constraints.
    :param h: Constants for inequality constraints.
    :param A: Coefficient matrix for equality constraints.
    :param b: Constants for equality constraints.
    :param max_iter: Maximum number of iterations.
    :param tol: Tolerance for convergence.
    :return: Optimal point \hat{x}.
    '''
    m, n = G.shape
    x = np.random.rand(n)   # Initial guess for x
    s = np.random.rand(m)   # Initial slack variables
    y = np.random.rand(A.shape[0])   # Dual variables for Ax = b
```

```
for _ in range(max_iter):
    mu = s.T @ s / m  # Complementarity measure
    if mu < tol:
        break

    # Residuals
    r_dual = c + G.T @ y - A.T @ s  # Dual residual
    r_cent = -np.linalg.multi_dot([x, s]) + mu * np.ones(m)  #
    ↪  Centrality residual
    r_pri = A @ x - b  # Primal residual

    # Solve Newton's system
    J = np.block([[np.zeros((n, n)), A.T, G.T],
                  [A, np.zeros((A.shape[0], A.shape[0])),
                   ↪  np.zeros((A.shape[0], m))],
                  [G, np.zeros((m, A.shape[0])), np.diag(s)]])

    r = np.concatenate([-r_dual, -r_pri, -r_cent])

    delta = np.linalg.solve(J, r)

    # Recover \delta_x, \delta_y, \delta_s
    delta_x = delta[:n]
    delta_y = delta[n:n + A.shape[0]]
    delta_s = delta[n + A.shape[0]:]

    # Line search and update
    alpha = 0.99
    x += alpha * delta_x
    y += alpha * delta_y
    s += alpha * delta_s

return x

# Example problem
c = np.array([1, 1, 0])
G = np.array([[-1, 1, 0],
              [1, -2, 0],
              [0, 0, -1]])
h = np.array([0, -1, 0])
A = np.array([[1, 1, 0]])
b = np.array([1])

optimal_x = interior_point_solver(c, G, h, A, b)
print("Optimal Solution:", optimal_x)
```

This code snippet defines a basic interior-point method for solving linear programming problems. Key functions and strategies implemented include:

- interior_point_solver function that applies the primal-dual path-following approach, solving a series of linear systems to update iterates.

- Calculation of residuals (r_dual, r_cent, r_pri) to measure optimality and feasibility.

- Construction and solution of the Jacobian system (J) to obtain search directions in primal and dual spaces.

- Line search strategy using the factor `alpha` to ensure convergence toward feasibility and optimality simultaneously.

The example provided uses a simple problem formulation to demonstrate the usage of the function and obtain an optimal solution.

Chapter 93

Seidel's Algorithm for Low-Dimensional Linear Programming

Below is a Python code snippet illustrating the implementation of Seidel's randomized linear programming algorithm in fixed dimensions, showcasing the incremental construction and expected linear-time performance aspect.

```python
import random
import numpy as np

def solve_lp(c, A, b):
    """
    Solves the linear programming problem:
    maximize c^T * x
    subject to A * x <= b and x >= 0
    using Seidel's randomized algorithm.

    :param c: Coefficients of the objective function.
    :param A: Constraint coefficients matrix.
    :param b: Constraint bounds vector.
    :return: Optimal solution vector x.
    """
    n, d = A.shape
    if n == 0:
        # No constraints, return x = 0
        return np.zeros(d)

    # Select random constraint
    k = random.randint(0, n - 1)
```

```
# Remove one constraint
A_ = np.delete(A, k, axis=0)
b_ = np.delete(b, k)

# Solve recursively the reduced problem
x = solve_lp(c, A_, b_)

if np.dot(A[k], x) <= b[k]:
    # If it satisfies, return the solution
    return x

# Recalculate with the violated constraint
A_k = A[k]
for i in range(d):
    if A_k[i] != 0:
        # Attempt to fix the constraint by modifying a variable
        A_k_div = A_k / A_k[i]
        b_k_div = b[k] / A_k[i]

        # New constraints
        A_new = np.append(A_, [-A_k_div], axis=0)
        b_new = np.append(b_, [-b_k_div])

        # Recursive call
        x_new = solve_lp(c, A_new, b_new)
        if x_new is not None:
            x[i] = b_k_div - np.dot(A_k_div, x_new)
            return x
return None


# Example of application
c = np.array([3, 2])  # The coefficients of the linear objective
↪   function
A = np.array([[1, -1], [-1, 1], [1, 0]])  # The coefficients matrix
↪   for constraints
b = np.array([1, 1, 2])  # The boundaries for constraints

opt_solution = solve_lp(c, A, b)  # Finding the optimal solution
print("Optimal Solution:", opt_solution)
```

This code defines the core components of Seidel's randomized algorithm for linear programming in fixed dimensions:

- `solve_lp` function implements the recursive procedure to solve linear programming problems by utilizing random constraint selection and recursive partitioning.

- The method leverages incremental construction to maximize the objective function c subject to constraints A and b, with expected linear-time performance.

- An example usage highlights the solution technique applied to a simple linear programming problem, assisting in comprehending both the utility and the efficiency of Seidel's algorithm.

This snippet thus demonstrates the practical application and efficiency gains of Seidel's approach in solving linear constraints, with emphasis on its probabilistic and recursive nature.

Chapter 94

Chan's Algorithm for Convex Hulls in 3D

Below is a Python code snippet that implements Chan's algorithm for computing the convex hulls in three dimensions. This implementation optimizes time complexity with an output-sensitive algorithmic approach.

```python
import numpy as np
from scipy.spatial import ConvexHull

def chan_3d(points):
    '''
    Implement Chan's algorithm for computing the convex hull of a
    ↪   set of 3D points.
    :param points: Numpy array of points with shape (n_points, 3).
    :return: Vertices of the convex hull.
    '''
    # Step 1: Initial partitioning of points
    def partition_points(points, m):
        return [points[i:i + m] for i in range(0, len(points), m)]

    # Step 2: Compute convex hull for each partitioned subset
    def compute_hull(points_subset):
        return ConvexHull(points_subset).vertices

    # Step 3: Combine hulls incrementally
    def combine_hulls(hull1, hull2):
        # Concatenate points and compute the hull again
        combined_points =
        ↪   np.concatenate((hull1.points[hull1.vertices],
        ↪   hull2.points[hull2.vertices]))
        return ConvexHull(combined_points)
```

```python
    # Set the chunk size based on the size of input
    m = int(np.ceil(np.sqrt(len(points))))
    subsets = partition_points(points, m)

    hulls = [compute_hull(subset) for subset in subsets]
    combined_hull = hulls[0]

    for i in range(1, len(hulls)):
        combined_hull = combine_hulls(combined_hull, hulls[i])

    return combined_hull.vertices

# Generate random 3D points
points = np.random.rand(30, 3)

# Compute the convex hull using Chan's algorithm
hull_vertices = chan_3d(points)
print("Vertices of the convex hull:", hull_vertices)

# Visualization (optional)
try:
    from mpl_toolkits.mplot3d import Axes3D
    import matplotlib.pyplot as plt

    fig = plt.figure()
    ax = fig.add_subplot(111, projection='3d')
    ax.scatter(points[:, 0], points[:, 1], points[:, 2],
    ↪  label='Points')

    # Draw the convex hull
    hull = ConvexHull(points)
    for simplex in hull.simplices:
        ax.plot(points[simplex, 0], points[simplex, 1],
        ↪  points[simplex, 2], 'k-')

    plt.title('3D Convex Hull using Chan\'s Algorithm')
    plt.legend()
    plt.show()
except ImportError:
    print("Visualization modules not available.")
```

This code defines key functions for the implementation of Chan's algorithm for computing 3D convex hulls:

- `partition_points` function divides the input points into smaller subsets of approximately equal size.

- `compute_hull` calculates the convex hull for a subset using the `ConvexHull` class from `scipy.spatial`.

- `combine_hulls` merges two hulls by recalculating the convex hull over their combined points, ensuring optimal output sensitivity.

The algorithm is designed to handle a variety of input sizes efficiently, leveraging the partition-compute-combine stages of Chan's method.

Chapter 95

Splay Trees: Self-Adjusting Binary Search Trees

Below is a Python code snippet that implements splay trees, focusing on key operations like rotations and splaying, which are fundamental in ensuring frequently accessed elements are moved closer to the root for improved average access time.

```python
class SplayTreeNode:
    def __init__(self, key, left=None, right=None):
        self.key = key
        self.left = left
        self.right = right

class SplayTree:
    def __init__(self):
        self.root = None

    def _right_rotate(self, x):
        y = x.left
        x.left = y.right
        y.right = x
        return y

    def _left_rotate(self, x):
        y = x.right
        x.right = y.left
        y.left = x
        return y
```

```python
    def _splay(self, root, key):
        if root is None or root.key == key:
            return root

        if root.key > key:
            if root.left is None:
                return root

            if root.left.key > key:
                root.left.left = self._splay(root.left.left, key)
                root = self._right_rotate(root)
            elif root.left.key < key:
                root.left.right = self._splay(root.left.right, key)
                if root.left.right is not None:
                    root.left = self._left_rotate(root.left)
            return root.left if root.left is None else
            ↪   self._right_rotate(root)
        else:
            if root.right is None:
                return root

            if root.right.key > key:
                root.right.left = self._splay(root.right.left, key)
                if root.right.left is not None:
                    root.right = self._right_rotate(root.right)
            elif root.right.key < key:
                root.right.right = self._splay(root.right.right,
                ↪   key)
                root = self._left_rotate(root)
            return root.right if root.right is None else
            ↪   self._left_rotate(root)

    def insert(self, key):
        if self.root is None:
            self.root = SplayTreeNode(key)
            return

        self.root = self._splay(self.root, key)

        if self.root.key == key:
            return

        new_node = SplayTreeNode(key)
        if self.root.key > key:
            new_node.right = self.root
            new_node.left = self.root.left
            self.root.left = None
        else:
            new_node.left = self.root
            new_node.right = self.root.right
            self.root.right = None

        self.root = new_node
```

```python
    def search(self, key):
        self.root = self._splay(self.root, key)
        return self.root is not None and self.root.key == key

    def delete(self, key):
        if self.root is None:
            return

        self.root = self._splay(self.root, key)

        if self.root.key != key:
            return

        if self.root.left is None:
            self.root = self.root.right
        else:
            temp = self.root
            self.root = self._splay(self.root.left, key)
            self.root.right = temp.right

# Example usage
splay_tree = SplayTree()
splay_tree.insert(10)
splay_tree.insert(20)
splay_tree.insert(30)
splay_tree.search(20)   # Splays the node with key 20 to the root
splay_tree.delete(10)
```

This code snippet encapsulates key operations and functionality of the splay tree:

- **SplayTreeNode**: Represents a node in the splay tree.

- **_right_rotate** and **_left_rotate**: Functions implementing right and left rotations, essential for tree rebalancing.

- **_splay**: The core splay function that adjusts the tree bringing a specified node to the root.

- **insert**: Handles insertion of a new key by first splaying the tree.

- **search**: Searches for a key in the tree, splaying the tree as necessary.

- **delete**: Removes a specified key, maintaining the splay tree properties.

These functions collaboratively ensure that frequently accessed elements are moved closer to the root of the tree, optimizing future access times through amortized analysis.

Chapter 96

Van Emde Boas Tree for Integer Key Storage

Below is a Python code snippet that illustrates the implementation of the Van Emde Boas tree, which supports dynamic operations in $O(\log \log n)$ time complexity by using recursive structures and bit manipulation techniques for integer key storage.

```python
class VanEmdeBoasTree:
    def __init__(self, universe_size):
        self.universe_size = universe_size
        self.min = None
        self.max = None

        if universe_size <= 2:
            self.summary = None
            self.cluster = [None] * universe_size
        else:
            self.lower_sqrt = 1 << (universe_size.bit_length() // 2)
            self.upper_sqrt = universe_size // self.lower_sqrt
            self.summary = VanEmdeBoasTree(self.upper_sqrt)
            self.cluster = [VanEmdeBoasTree(self.lower_sqrt) for _
            ↪  in range(self.upper_sqrt)]

    def high(self, x):
        return x // self.lower_sqrt

    def low(self, x):
        return x % self.lower_sqrt

    def index(self, x, y):
        return x * self.lower_sqrt + y
```

```
def member(self, x):
    if x == self.min or x == self.max:
        return True
    elif self.universe_size == 2:
        return False
    else:
        return self.cluster[self.high(x)].member(self.low(x))

def insert(self, x):
    if self.min is None:
        self.min = self.max = x
    else:
        if x < self.min:
            x, self.min = self.min, x
        if self.universe_size > 2:
            if self.cluster[self.high(x)].min is None:
                self.summary.insert(self.high(x))
                self.cluster[self.high(x)].min =
                ↪   self.cluster[self.high(x)].max = self.low(x)
            else:
                self.cluster[self.high(x)].insert(self.low(x))
        if x > self.max:
            self.max = x

def delete(self, x):
    if self.min == self.max:
        self.min = self.max = None
    elif self.universe_size == 2:
        if x == 0:
            self.min = 1
        else:
            self.min = 0
        self.max = self.min
    else:
        if x == self.min:
            first_cluster = self.summary.min
            x = self.index(first_cluster,
            ↪   self.cluster[first_cluster].min)
            self.min = x
        self.cluster[self.high(x)].delete(self.low(x))
        if self.cluster[self.high(x)].min is None:
            self.summary.delete(self.high(x))
            if x == self.max:
                summary_max = self.summary.max
                if summary_max is None:
                    self.max = self.min
                else:
                    self.max = self.index(summary_max,
                    ↪   self.cluster[summary_max].max)
        elif x == self.max:
            self.max = self.index(self.high(x),
            ↪   self.cluster[self.high(x)].max)
```

```
# Example Usage
vEB = VanEmdeBoasTree(16)
vEB.insert(2)
vEB.insert(3)
vEB.insert(10)

print("3 is a member:", vEB.member(3))   # True
print("5 is a member:", vEB.member(5))   # False

vEB.delete(3)
print("3 is a member after deletion:", vEB.member(3))   # False
```

This code defines a `VanEmdeBoasTree` class which supports efficient operations on a set of integer keys:

- `__init__` initializes a Van Emde Boas tree with the given universe size, setting up the structure for handling base cases and recursive clusters.

- `high`, `low`, and `index` functions perform bit manipulation to extract or combine high and low parts of an integer key.

- `member` checks the existence of a key, exploiting stored minimum and maximum values for quick checks before diving into recursive clusters.

- `insert` adds a key to the structure, updating the minimum, maximum, and necessary clusters, along with the summary structure.

- `delete` removes a key efficiently by adjusting pointers and simplifying the structure where necessary.

Chapter 97

Hough Transform for Feature Extraction

Below is a Python code snippet that demonstrates the usage of the Hough Transform algorithm for detecting lines and circles in an image. This script leverages the 'cv2' module from OpenCV for image processing operations.

```python
import cv2
import numpy as np

def detect_lines(image_path, rho=1, theta=np.pi/180, threshold=100):
    '''
    Detect lines in an image using Hough Transform.
    :param image_path: Path to the input image.
    :param rho: Distance resolution of the accumulator in pixels.
    :param theta: Angle resolution of the accumulator in radians.
    :param threshold: Accumulator threshold parameter. Only lines
    ↪   with enough votes are returned.
    :return: Image with detected lines.
    '''
    img = cv2.imread(image_path, cv2.IMREAD_COLOR)
    gray = cv2.cvtColor(img, cv2.COLOR_BGR2GRAY)
    edges = cv2.Canny(gray, 50, 150, apertureSize=3)

    lines = cv2.HoughLines(edges, rho, theta, threshold)
    if lines is not None:
        for line in lines:
            rho, theta = line[0]
            a = np.cos(theta)
            b = np.sin(theta)
            x0 = a * rho
            y0 = b * rho
```

```
                x1 = int(x0 + 1000 * (-b))
                y1 = int(y0 + 1000 * (a))
                x2 = int(x0 - 1000 * (-b))
                y2 = int(y0 - 1000 * (a))
                cv2.line(img, (x1, y1), (x2, y2), (0, 0, 255), 2)

    return img

def detect_circles(image_path, dp=1.2, min_dist=100, param1=100,
↪    param2=30, min_radius=0, max_radius=0):
    '''
    Detect circles in an image using Hough Transform.
    :param image_path: Path to the input image.
    :param dp: Inverse ratio of the accumulator resolution to the
    ↪    image resolution.
    :param min_dist: Minimum distance between the centers of the
    ↪    detected circles.
    :param param1: Higher threshold for the Canny edge detector
    ↪    (lower threshold is half).
    :param param2: Accumulator threshold for the circle centers at
    ↪    the detection stage.
    :param min_radius: Minimum circle radius.
    :param max_radius: Maximum circle radius.
    :return: Image with detected circles.
    '''
    img = cv2.imread(image_path, cv2.IMREAD_COLOR)
    gray = cv2.cvtColor(img, cv2.COLOR_BGR2GRAY)
    gray = cv2.medianBlur(gray, 5)

    circles = cv2.HoughCircles(gray, cv2.HOUGH_GRADIENT, dp,
    ↪    min_dist,
                               param1=param1, param2=param2,
                               ↪    minRadius=min_radius,
                               ↪    maxRadius=max_radius)

    if circles is not None:
        circles = np.uint16(np.around(circles))
        for i in circles[0, :]:
            center = (i[0], i[1])
            # circle center
            cv2.circle(img, center, 1, (0, 100, 100), 3)
            # circle outline
            radius = i[2]
            cv2.circle(img, center, radius, (255, 0, 255), 3)

    return img

# Example usage:
# Output images can be displayed using cv2.imshow or saved using
↪    cv2.imwrite
line_image = detect_lines('lines_input.jpg')
cv2.imwrite('lines_output.jpg', line_image)
```

```
circle_image = detect_circles('circles_input.jpg')
cv2.imwrite('circles_output.jpg', circle_image)
```

This code defines key functions for detecting geometric features in images using the Hough Transform:

- `detect_lines` function utilizes the Hough Line Transform to detect lines in an image. It takes parameters like 'rho', 'theta', and 'threshold' to configure the line detection sensitivity.

- `detect_circles` employs the Hough Circle Transform to find circular features, allowing customization of detection parameters including 'dp', 'min_dist', 'param1', 'param2', 'min_radius', and 'max_radius'.

To execute the code, ensure to have the required Python packages installed, and provide the appropriate input image paths. The output images, with detected features, can either be displayed or saved using relevant OpenCV functions.

Chapter 98

Dynamic Time Warping Algorithm for Time Series Analysis

Below is a Python code snippet that implements the Dynamic Time Warping (DTW) algorithm, which measures similarity between two temporal sequences. This implementation computes the optimal alignment path and applies the algorithm in areas such as speech and pattern recognition.

```python
import numpy as np

def dtw(sequence_a, sequence_b):
    """
    Computes the Dynamic Time Warping distance between two
    ↪    sequences.

    :param sequence_a: First sequence to compare.
    :param sequence_b: Second sequence to compare.
    :return: A tuple containing the DTW distance and the optimal
    ↪    path.
    """
    len_a, len_b = len(sequence_a), len(sequence_b)
    # Initialize the cost matrix with infinity
    cost_matrix = np.full((len_a + 1, len_b + 1), np.inf)
    cost_matrix[0, 0] = 0

    # Compute cumulative cost matrix
    for i in range(1, len_a + 1):
        for j in range(1, len_b + 1):
```

```
                    cost = abs(sequence_a[i-1] - sequence_b[j-1])
                    cost_matrix[i, j] = cost + min(cost_matrix[i-1, j],      #
                    ↪   Insertion

                                               cost_matrix[i, j-1],      #
                                               ↪   Deletion
                                               cost_matrix[i-1, j-1])   #
                                               ↪   Match


    # Trace back the optimal path
    path = []
    i, j = len_a, len_b
    while i > 0 or j > 0:
        path.append((i - 1, j - 1))
        if i == 0:
            j -= 1
        elif j == 0:
            i -= 1
        else:
            prev_costs = [cost_matrix[i-1, j], cost_matrix[i, j-1],
            ↪   cost_matrix[i-1, j-1]]
            step = np.argmin(prev_costs)
            if step == 0:
                i -= 1
            elif step == 1:
                j -= 1
            else:
                i -= 1
                j -= 1
    path.reverse()

    return cost_matrix[len_a, len_b], path

# Example sequences
sequence_a = [1, 3, 4, 9]
sequence_b = [1, 4, 9]

# Calculating DTW distance and optimal path
dtw_distance, optimal_path = dtw(sequence_a, sequence_b)

print("DTW Distance:", dtw_distance)
print("Optimal Path:", optimal_path)
```

This code defines the key functions required for computing the
Dynamic Time Warping (DTW) distance and the optimal alignment path between two sequences:

- `dtw` function calculates the DTW distance using a cost matrix to measure similarity, allowing for elastic shifts in time,
  which is particularly useful in comparing time series that may
  exhibit out-of-sync patterns.

- The cost matrix is initialized with infinity to satisfy boundary conditions, and the algorithm iteratively builds the matrix leveraging a dynamic programming approach.

- It also includes backtracking to derive the optimal path for alignment, providing insight into how one sequence can be warped into another.

The code ends with an example that computes the DTW distance and optimal path for two sample sequences, illustrating the application of this method in real-world scenarios like speech recognition or pattern matching.

Chapter 99

Expectation-Maximization Algorithm for Parameter Estimation

Below is a Python code snippet that encompasses the key computational elements of the Expectation-Maximization (EM) algorithm, including initialization, expectation and maximization steps, and convergence checks for parameter estimation in statistical models with latent variables.

```python
import numpy as np

def initialize_parameters(K, n_features):
    """
    Initialize the parameters for the Gaussian Mixture Model.
    :param K: Number of clusters.
    :param n_features: Dimensionality of the data.
    :return: Initial weights, means, and covariances.
    """
    weights = np.ones(K) / K
    means = np.random.rand(K, n_features)
    covariances = np.array([np.eye(n_features) for _ in range(K)])
    return weights, means, covariances

def e_step(X, weights, means, covariances):
    """
    Perform the expectation step.
```

```
    :param X: Data points.
    :param weights: Current weights for each mixture component.
    :param means: Mean vectors for each component.
    :param covariances: Covariance matrices for each component.
    :return: Responsibility matrix.
    """
    N, _ = X.shape
    K = weights.size
    responsibilities = np.zeros((N, K))

    for k in range(K):
        responsibilities[:, k] = weights[k] *
        ↪  multivariate_normal.pdf(X, mean=means[k],
        ↪  cov=covariances[k])

    responsibilities = responsibilities /
    ↪  responsibilities.sum(axis=1, keepdims=True)
    return responsibilities

def m_step(X, responsibilities):
    """
    Perform the maximization step.
    :param X: Data points.
    :param responsibilities: Responsibility matrix.
    :return: Updated weights, means, and covariances.
    """
    Nk = responsibilities.sum(axis=0)
    weights = Nk / X.shape[0]
    means = np.dot(responsibilities.T, X) / Nk[:, None]
    covariances = np.zeros((weights.size, X.shape[1], X.shape[1]))

    for k in range(weights.size):
        X_centered = X - means[k]
        covariances[k] = np.dot(responsibilities[:, k] *
        ↪  X_centered.T, X_centered) / Nk[k]

    return weights, means, covariances

def em_algorithm(X, K, max_iter=100, tol=1e-6):
    """
    Execute the Expectation-Maximization algorithm.
    :param X: Data points.
    :param K: Number of clusters/components.
    :param max_iter: Maximum number of iterations.
    :param tol: Convergence tolerance.
    :return: Final parameter estimates.
    """
    n_features = X.shape[1]
    weights, means, covariances = initialize_parameters(K,
    ↪  n_features)

    log_likelihood = 0
    for iteration in range(max_iter):
```

```
old_log_likelihood = log_likelihood

# E-step
responsibilities = e_step(X, weights, means, covariances)

# M-step
weights, means, covariances = m_step(X, responsibilities)

# Check for convergence
log_likelihood = np.sum(np.log(np.sum([w *
↪    multivariate_normal.pdf(X, mean=mu, cov=cov)
                                    for w, mu, cov in
                                        ↪    zip(weights,
                                        ↪    means,
                                        ↪    covariances)],
                                        ↪    axis=0)))
if abs(log_likelihood - old_log_likelihood) < tol:
    break

    return weights, means, covariances, log_likelihood

# Example usage
from scipy.stats import multivariate_normal

# Simulated data
X = np.random.rand(100, 2)
K = 3

weights, means, covariances, log_likelihood = em_algorithm(X, K)
print("Final weights:", weights)
print("Final means:", means)
print("Final covariances:", covariances)
```

This code defines several key functions necessary for the implementation and operation of the Expectation-Maximization algorithm:

- `initialize_parameters` function initializes the parameters of the Gaussian Mixture Model including weights, means, and covariances.

- `e_step` calculates the expectation step, returning the responsibility matrix which indicates how much each data point belongs to each cluster.

- `m_step` performs the maximization step, updating the parameters based on the current responsibilities.

- `em_algorithm` orchestrates the EM process by iteratively performing E-step and M-step, checking for convergence with respect to the change in log-likelihood.

The final block of code provides an example of using these functions with simulated data for clustering via a Gaussian Mixture Model.